SOCIAL STRESS
AND
MENTAL HEALTH

SOCIAL STRESS
AND
MENTAL HEALTH

A Social-Psychiatric Field Study of Calcutta

AJITA CHAKRABORTY

Sage Publications
New Delhi/Newbury Park/London

Copyright © Ajita Chakraborty, 1990

First published in 1990 by

Sage Publications India Pvt Ltd
32 M Block Market, Greater Kailash I
New Delhi 110 048

Sage Publications Inc
2111 West Hillcrest Drive
Newbury Park, California 91320

Sage Publications Ltd
28 Banner Street
London EC1Y 8QE

Published by Tejeshwar Singh for Sage Publications India Pvt Ltd, phototypeset by Mudra Typesetters, Pondicherry and printed at Chaman Offset Printers, Delhi.

Library of Congress Cataloging-in-Publication Data

Chakraborty, Ajita.
 Social stress and mental health: a social psychiatric field study of Calcutta/ Ajita Chakraborty.
  p. cm.
 Includes bibliographical references.
  1. Mental   illness—India—Calcutta. 2. Urbanization—India—Calcutta—Psychological   aspects. 3. Industrialization—India—Calcutta—Psychological aspects. 4. Mental health surveys—India—Calcutta. I. Title.
  [DNLM: 1. Mental Disorders—epidemiology—India. 2. Socioeconomic Factors.]
 RC451.I42C343 1990 362.2'0422'0954147—dc20 DNLM/DLC 89-70176

ISBN: 0-8039-9633-0 (hbk.—USA)
    81-7036-180-X (hbk.—India)

Dedicated to the Memory of the late
PROFESSOR H.B.M. MURPHY
M.D., Ph.D. McGill University, Canada

Who contributed more than anyone else
to the stimulation and training of researchers
in psychiatry in the Third World

Contents

List of Tables

Preface

THE mere word 'mental' is usually equated with gross mental disorders by the public and everybody is avidly curious to know what causes such disorders. To psychiatrists mental disorders are of various types, shades and grades; there are no ready answers as to the causation. Today, it is believed that mental disorders occur through combinations and interactions of several factors: biological, psychological and socio-cultural. Biological vulnerability can exist independently through malfunctioning of the biochemical systems in the body, or through faulty genetic control of those systems. Physical diseases, deficiencies and infections can also cause mental disorders. Psychological stresses can occur through dysfunctional interpersonal relationships or through as yet uncharted processes. Socio-cultural factors are also recognised to be extremely important in causing psychological stresses in an indirect way.

We will give here a very brief outline of the most important socio-logical factors (cultural factors being covered within the text), namely, industrialisation and urbanisation in the context of mental health. The rationale for this is that these conditions have always been thought to exert profound influence on mental health. Though the present study did not set out to discern these effects, it was nevertheless conducted within those perspectives.

Toffler's outstanding book *Future Shock* (1970) has drawn the attention of the thinking public to the possible catastrophe that the world may be threatened by if social change of the type we are experiencing now is allowed to continue unchecked. This social change has been brought about by rapid technological advancement; a process which started with the industrial revolution in Europe.

Since India, in contrast to the developed nations of the West, is still in the process of developing its industries, we prefer to discuss the subject of mental health in relation to industrialisation and urbanisation, rather than to the technological revolution. The vast sociological area of social change is in any case quite beyond our scope.

It is a truism to state that industrialisation brings in its wake untold misery and suffering before the beneficial effects are realised. The effects of the industrial revolution in Britain have remained like scars in the annals of her history even though the process ushered in the modern era of progress and prosperity. Industrialisation changed societies, human relationships and values on which the world had rested for hundreds of years. Of course this was not due to the growth of industries alone; there were many other factors which changed every facet of human life in the last two centuries.

Most of these changes have been thought to be detrimental to the quality of life, material prosperity notwithstanding. The changes involved concepts of time—the change from a slow paced, leisurely rural rhythm to a fast, ever-changing, hurried, time-bound city life. The economic order changed to make man depend on the insecurity of wages and jobs instead of living on the fruits of his own labour and being part of a natural process. In the wake of these changes hundreds of thousands of people left their land and villages and moved into cities giving rise to squalid slums, poverty, misery, tension and strife. Revolutions changing the political order followed in many places. Even in capitalist countries reforms forced the situation to improve; welfare states came into being; food, health and sanitation became available to all. The upswing of prosperity with occasional fluctuations has continued in the western world for decades with the ever increasing development of industry and technology.

In the west the earlier problems of industrialisation have disappeared or have lessened and rural migration has also stopped. However, other subtle but more devastating changes have occurred. Families, having been reduced to ever smaller units, are threatening to disappear altogether. There is less cohesiveness within social groups. There are feelings of rootlessness, of not belonging, of alienation, and a felt need to 'search for identity' is rampant. Great wars have been fought between nations, but disputes show no signs of abating and nations remain poised for mutual destruction and total annihilation of life and civilisation.

Like all other Third World countries India has embarked on a relentless endeavour to industrialise, since its independence from British rule, in an effort to feed a huge population and to combat poverty. Partly because of the pre-existing miserable conditions and partly because of the country's immense size and diverse modes of living, the effects that can be solely attributed to industrialisation remain to be delineated. However, one process that is unmistakable, fairly recent and alarming is rural-to-urban migration. Perhaps, at the risk of over-simplification, this might be due to industrialisation though a host of other factor are involved. There is no doubt, nevertheless, that urbanisation is producing immense stress on both immigrants and city dwellers.

The change from rural to city life, to judge from individual experiences, causes stresses and strains and it has always been thought that these give rise to mental ill-health. It was once conjectured that there would be less mental illness in uncomplicated, simple rural people than in strife-torn, tension ridden city dwellers. But many of these assumptions have not been borne out by field studies. Many of these studies have shown that the apparently tension free rural communities also have their share of mental disorders at comparable rates. But the concepts involved in these areas of study have changed.

Many conditions, such as crime, delinquency, drug addiction or personality disorders, were not always thought of as psychiatric problems. The association of these conditions with the urban environment is obvious, but their status within a medical discipline remains dubious. The point is, however, that though it has not been possible to directly link medically diagnosable mental disorders to good or bad social conditions, such hypotheses have not entirely been refuted. The whole controversial area requires clarification from different viewpoints.

Few studies have been conducted in developing countries where processes of change may be manifest in different ways. In India, urban studies from the point of view of mental health have been negligible. The present work is the only one to date of any magnitude and depth. It was conducted with standard epidemiological methods but, as stated earlier, only the perspective of social change was kept in mind; the sections of the population which are particularly vulnerable to these processes were given special attention as were certain structural elements of society, for example, the family. What has been gathered implicates industrialisation and urbanisation only indirectly, but it is hoped that the study will form a baseline for the detection of the effects of further change.

In addition to this, another outlook is implicit in the study. The author, as an adherent of the existential phenomenological school, holds that the claim of psychiatry as an objective science is not tenable, and that philosophical trends and numerous biases are present in psychiatric theories which influence even such practical issues as the making of diagnosis. Uncritical application of concepts and categories developed in the West to Indian psychiatry, which is still at an observational, fact gathering stage, will be detrimental to its development. The present study was launched on the conviction that it is better to record accurate observations rather than err towards misdirected scientific endeavour. It made the work archaic but genuine.

Acknowledgements

THE hazards through which this survey passed and finally saw print are beyond description and it would be better not to pursue that subject. The completion of the project was made possible through generous help and voluntary assistance from friends and in particular students who were associated with the project at various stages. The untiring efforts of Dr. B. Sandel, Consultant Psychiatrist, Severalls Hospital, UK, during the planning, fieldwork and first phase analysis, and the seminal help with the computer work by Baladev Basu, Computer Scientist, Indian Institute of Management, Calcutta were the two most significant contributions. Dr. Chandak Sengoopta, Cornell University, USA, took painstaking care over the manuscript. Dr. Erna Hoch, previously Professor of Psychiatry at AIIMS, Delhi and WHO Advisor, read the manuscript and made several valuable corrections. For all of this assistance I express my deepest gratitude.

It was my misfortune that Dr. H.B.M. Murphy, to whom the book is dedicated, did not live to see the work completed. Without his support, encouragement and help I could not have pursued whatever research I have done.

My sincere thanks are also due to Dr. Bivas Roy Chowdhury, Dr. Rahul Mukherji, Sri Ajit Mukherji, Mrs. Anita Sengupta, Dr. Debashis Bhattacharya, Dr. Soumitra Basu, Dr. Bappaditya Dev, Dr. K.L. Narayanan, Dr. Jayanti Basu, Sri Subhas Biswas, Mr. Sanat Kar, Dr. Dipankar Mukherji, Dr. Jayanta Chatterji, Mrs. Bonani Kakkar, Mr. Subhankar Mukherji, Dr. Monisha Sen, Dr. Anjali Sengupta, Amar Dutta, D.K. Basu and Amit Roy of the Data Processing Services Ltd.; and to the Indian Council of Medical Research for funding the second phase analysis. Thanks are also due to the field investigators who executed the arduous fieldwork with honesty and sincerity and to the citizens of Calcutta whose co-operation went beyond our expectations.

Ajita Chakraborty

— 1 —

Introduction

IN the late seventies, a comprehensive health and socio-economic survey of Calcutta and its environs was conducted by the Calcutta Metropolitan Development Authority, in collaboration with the Health Department of the Government of West Bengal and the Indian Statistical Institute. The mental health study was conducted as an independent part of this survey. We may qualify the foregoing statement by saying that the mental health aspect was originally envisaged by the authorities to be a minor part of the health survey, but it eventually became fairly extensive and a survey in its own right. We had joined the survey with much misgiving, thinking that there would be too many constraints and perhaps, the basic requirements of a psychiatric survey would not be met, but we also realised that here was once in a lifetime opportunity to learn about and record some part of life in Calcutta as it was in the late seventies. We took it upon ourselves to make the best of this opportunity and conduct the first ever major mental health survey in Calcutta. The authorities gave us complete freedom within certain constraints of funds, infrastructure and sampling. A lot of improvisation was done at a personal cost to maintain the boundaries of the mental health survey within its technical parameters but with a bias towards the social aspects. It took us some years of intense involvement to complete the task.

Being part of a comprehensive health survey, the mental health survey benefited in every way, namely, access to 'difficult' areas, adequate health information regarding our sample, and detailed information on the socio-economic conditions of the whole population. These provided us with the most important demographic correlates. Isolated psychiatric surveys are usually confined to limited areas, whereas in this case, the basic sample, common to both the surveys, was spread over a large area. This aspect of the sampling made the task arduous, but it encompassed the complexity and inherent variety of Calcutta. A smaller study with greater emphasis on diagnostic sophistication (a dubious venture in any case) would have lost the general feel of life of the population at the time.

It is accepted that there are few actual records or hard data on society, family, economics and the physical or mental health of the people of Calcutta. For first hand accounts of people's difficulties in conducting their daily life, we have either literature or journalistic accounts. Anthropological or sociological studies invariably avoid the psychological dimensions. From that point of view, our raw data and interviews are worthy of preservation for posterity. It might be asked whether such data could be considered to constitute a true indicator of mental health. The answer depends on what mental health is considered to be.

In a paper on the subject of mental health, Chakraborty (1967) declared that there was no such thing as mental health, and this was before the anti-psychiatry movement appeared on the scene! However, it was apparent, as eminent social scientists had been pointing out from the very beginning of the mental hygiene movement, that the phrase 'mental health' had neither any precise meaning nor did it signify any definite category (Wootton, 1959).

It is for its very ambiguity that this term is being used in the present title. Mental health broadly implies the existence of a psychiatric disorder, illness and also much more, it includes people's subjective stresses, joys, sorrows and what is now fashionably called 'the quality of life.'

'Mental health' as a field of study by common usage is taken to be the same as psychiatry or psychological medicine. The model followed in psychiatry is similar to that of any other medical discipline. Its essential concern is with ill health: the diagnosis and treatment of patients.

It is rather startling to note that there is no unanimously accepted definition for health. The WHO definition stating that 'health is a state of complete physical, mental and social well-being and not merely the absence of disease or infirmity' (WHO, 1948), has not been made operational. No criteria have been evolved to estimate 'well-being'. 'As a result we tend to describe and measure health as obverse of disease, illness, disability' (Susser, 1973). This 'measure' is not only of the sick who consult doctors or attend hospitals, because all sick people do not do so. One, therefore, needs to examine both the sick and the healthy directly among the general population. Such procedures constitute a separate branch of medicine known as epidemiology which is 'the study of the distribution and determinants of diseases and injuries in human population . . . .' Epidemiology is concerned with the extent and types of illnesses and injuries in groups of people and with the factors which influence their distribution. 'Disease is not randomly distributed throughout a population, but rather that subgroups differ in the frequency of different diseases . . . knowledge of this uneven distribution can be used to investigate etiologic [causative] factors and to lay the groundwork for programs of prevention and control' (Mausner and Bahn, 1974).

Epidemiological concepts and methods are applicable to mental health. However, mental disorders are comparatively rare and field surveys are extremely difficult and expensive in terms of money, energy and other resources. Consequently, other avenues to determine the extent and distribution of mental diseases have been explored. Some of these involve the study of old official health records, mental hospital admission rates, records of general practitioners, etc. It is well known that such data may be biased unless they are extremely thorough and comprehensive covering the whole population of a defined area. Collection of data by these methods is feasible only in some western countries, where extensive personal and health information of all the individuals in a population are obtainable through health and welfare agencies. The rest of the world has to depend on field surveys for the estimation of morbidity (disease rates), or on censuses for other information.

Mental disorders do not produce high mortality (except a proportion of suicides) but do give rise to high morbidity, which implies debility or disability.

So far we have been talking of health in a global sense, and not of individual diseases. However, mental disorders are subdivided into several diseases or classified into a pattern (based mainly on similarities in the manifestation and outcome). Of these, the 'psychoses' group represents the 'major illnesses', with poor outcome and great disability. The other, much larger group constitutes the 'psychoneuroses', or 'minor illnesses', so to speak, which involve much suffering but less disability. Psychoses are further divided into schizophrenia, affective disorders, organic psychoses, etc. Schizophrenia is assumed to be the most important of the mental diseases because it has an extremely poor prognosis (or outcome) as compared to others. From the point of view of public health, it is the chronic disabling conditions (requiring state aided treatment through hospitals, rehabilitation centres, etc.) which deserve maximum attention. Mental retardation is another condition where amelioration is not very effective, especially in severe cases. These cases eventually become the responsibility of the state. Persons suffering from neuroses do not usually lose their working capacity and hence are rarely 'social liabilities'. However, the conditions, particularly the ever increasing 'anxiety depression' variety, are probably linked with socio-cultural causative factors and deserve our urgent concern. Apart from the conditions mentioned above, there are other groups and conditions, such as, abnormal personality, psycho-pathy (including criminals, addicts, and the unduly aggressive people), senile deterioration, epilepsy and a few others which are important constituents of the psychiatric spectrum.

To determine the extent of mental ill health, we look for these conditions in the population. However, this search is complicated by two problems: detection of a case and its diagnosis.

A suspected patient or 'case' has to be referred to a doctor to achieve that status. Referral may be through relatives, neighbours, an official agency, or the patient himself. In the case of psychotics, or the mentally retarded or for all childhood disorders, it is nearly always the other people who identify the sick. Problems arise in the case of minor psychiatric disorders (psychoneuroses) and in the diagnosis of sub-types of psychoses. Psychoneuroses are not recognised by all people as conditions which can be complained of, and the dividing line between normal variations and the pathological is unclear. So, how should a 'case' of neurosis be identified? This is an issue which is being ex-tensively studied and debated. For that matter, it may be very difficult to diagnose different psychotic states. (Both these points will be discussed later). Yet, these problems are crucial. Many like Shepherd (1977) feel that psychiatry must move beyond the 'layman's model of madness', and be able to recognise that neurosis is as much a sickness as psychosis.

To deal with such problems, various tests, scales and instruments have been devised. Since trained manpower, that is, research psychia-trists are always in short supply everywhere, the aim is to obtain the diagnosis through these tests which can be administered by less expert staff. But the tests so far devised are not entirely suitable for field studies or for diverse and differing conditions. Most surveys, therefore, devise their own instruments and adopt methods of their own choice.

As a result, the findings of different studies are seldom strictly comparable. The aim of all research is communication through comparability, but in psychiatry it has not yet been possible to introduce standardised and universally accepted methods. Every new survey severely criticises the previous ones and claims scientific rigour for its own method, only to be supplanted by others. Perhaps, the lesson to be learnt from this is that local conditions impose severe limitations and the best methods are not always applicable. Hence there is little scope to be rigid.

Examples of a few surveys (among scores) will serve to illustrate this point. Estimating mental ill health by examining official records, including those of general practitioners, has already been mentioned. Such 'case register' studies are only possible where each and every case gets recorded by some agency. They also require fairly extensive documentation of the whole population. Of the actual field studies (which seek to identify cases in the population), one of the notable surveys in the west is the 'Midtown Manhattan Study' (Srole *et al.*, 1962). A large number of households in the Manhattan area of New York were visited by trained assistants (under the guidance of psychiatrists and sociologists) and questionnaires were filled out by them. Psychiatrists later graded the answers into different categories of disabilities. No diagnoses were made. Both the methodology and the findings of this study have been severely criticised because they were not found to be comparable to those of other psychiatric surveys. Nevertheless, this study remains a landmark and is one of the very few studies that have been conducted in large, densely populated, industrial and urban areas.

A study along similar lines in Kota, a village in South India, by Carstairs and Kapur (1976), also came under severe criticism. If disability is determined only on the basis of the symptoms elicited by the questionnaire, very high figures of morbidity are obtained, which do not convince clinicians as being an accurate reflection of the true state of affairs.

In developing countries the most popular strategy has been to conduct a two-stage study. In the first stage the assistants seek out the patients, who are then diagnosed by psychiatrists usually in a different setting (a clinic, for instance). Apart from Lin's (1953) study in Taiwan, areas covered by Asian or Indian studies have been small and restricted either to rural areas, towns or small cities (like Lucknow, Sethi *et al.*, 1967; 1974). This method is dependent on the knowledge and motive of the suppliers of the initial information, sensitivity of the assistants and other similar factors (Murphy, 1982).

Another method used abroad is that of direct case identification with the help of a specially constructed questionnaire (symptom check-list) which is administered by trained personnel to all persons in a defined area. Though this method eliminates many kinds of bias, yet it is not suitable for psychotics, mentally retarded and uncooperative persons in general. Yet another strategy involves the employment of a short standardised instrument (test) for direct use in the field, or asking 'suspect' cases to come to the clinic for detailed examination. The method is expensive and requires abundant trained manpower. Also, the aim of these methods is to make accurate diagnosis for research purposes.

Psychiatry is riddled with a great many controversies, but for practical difficulties, some of which have been elaborated earlier, the choice or option of methods to resolve them are very few. Whether one agrees with the so-called medical model or not, it is the only course through which communicable working methods can be established. For the present study we have followed the conventional forms, ideas and concepts, but some innovative methods have been used and emphasis has been placed on how people view mental problems. The words (not medical terms) they use to describe these, the vernacular equivalents of certain conditions and the 'folk' ideas of mental illness (we believe that folk concepts very often embody basic existential truths), to form an idea of their perception of mental health.

Concepts of 'madness' ('*mathar golmal*', '*pagol*') in Bengali culture, both conceptually and attributionally, are the same as elsewhere (Bhattacharya, 1986) although labelling depends on many different factors. Possibly such labelled persons are only the confirmed and chronic cases, comprising a narrow range of psychotics. However, this approach makes it possible to detect a wide range of behaviour anomalies which may not come to the doctor's attention and remain forever outside the diagnostic spectrum. Many categories where cultural and medical concepts overlap (Leighton *et al.*, 1963a) were sought out and confirmed. Beyond the accepted and labelled categories, people's distress, the commonly expressed 'neurotic' complaints were also enquired into. We do not claim that the subjective experience of distress could be accurately gauged, we could only record what the people chose to communicate.

It is understood that vague and random complaints or impressionistic opinion even from an expert do not reveal anything. Social labelling or oddities of behaviour do not merit an expensive, large-scale survey. For such matters to indicate social malaise or ill health or to have social relevance, some criterion is required. 'Need for help' on the basis of impairment of social functioning is usually taken as one such criterion. We did take this into account, though in an indirect way, which will be explained later. It should be appreciated that a field survey in a large and overcrowded city, particularly on a sensitive subject like psychological problems, was an immensely difficult task, often bordering on danger. If a far more sensitive element, like ability to work (to judge 'social dysfunction') was to be added, the population could turn uncooperative. Such surveys also raise the question of ethics. To quote Murphy (1982) who has conducted a large number of surveys both in Canada and in developing countries:

> In nearly all field health surveys, certain expectations are raised in the minds of those interviewed . . . and it is both dishonest and often harmful if these expectations cannot be met . . . there is some evidence that such a survey may turn the minds of the respondents away from traditional style of complaint and sources of help toward new symptoms and to services which may not be available.

Before concluding this brief introduction to psychiatric surveys, the aim of epidemiology needs to be re-stated. It not only seeks to ascertain the extent of disease but also to explore the factors in the environment which may be causally linked with the disease. It is an established fact that different sub-groups vary amongst each other in their disease proneness as, for instance, women or the aged. These vulnerable groups need to be identified, because the final aim is the control of disease and its prevention.

The usual demographic, social and ecological factors that are believed to be associated with psychiatric disorders are age, sex, economic conditions, education, occupation, social class, social mobility, density of habitat, addictions, family pattern or structure, work and recreation (conditions and opportunities), trauma, injuries, mother's health and pregnancy, the subject's health, diet, etc.

By themselves these factors are not causal, but they interact with other such factors as genetic, psychological and social to give rise to disorders in predisposed individuals.

2

Methodology of the Field Survey

PREAMBLE

THE Calcutta Metropolitan Development Authority conducted a large scale health and socio-economic survey of the city and the outlying areas under its jurisdiction comprising over 10 million people. The survey was conducted under the joint auspices of the CMDA, the Indian Statistical Institute and the Health Department of West Bengal Government.

The general health and socio-economic survey was conducted by one group of investigators. The mental health survey was conducted by another group of investigators. Both groups were placed under the supervision of the same medical officer when the basic data were collected. After the completion of the first phase of the field work, the mental health staff worked independently.

The sampling design and sample units were common to the general health and socio-economic survey and the mental health survey. The sampling design and the selection of sample was done by the Indian Statistical Institute, however it was not involved with the rest of the work for the mental health survey.

Though the basic demographic data collected by the mental health section were identical to those of the other teams, these were collected separately. Data pertaining to family expenditure was not collected by the mental health section but obtained from the socio-economic section. The physical health of individuals was also not examined by the mental health section. Information about the health of the respondents was obtained from the data already collected by the team of doctors, and was recorded in the mental health schedules.

Data collection was completed by the end of 1978, and the CMDA published its final report in 1983. Later permission was obtained and a grant was provided by the Indian Council of Medical Research to the author for completion of the mental health study. The present work is based on an analysis of data, which differs from the original (as published in the CMDA Report, 1983) in some respects. Nearly 1,000 individuals who were initially included as 'casual' (that is, not usual) members of the family were dropped from the sample of the mental health study. Data about such people were clearly demarcated during collection, hence their later exclusion did not affect the main findings. Economic groupings were also changed by taking different cut-off points for the present study.

The Institute of Postgraduate Medical Education and Research, Calcutta, remained the main centre during the entire period of this work.

OPERATIONAL PROCEDURE

Nearly fifty trained personnel were involved in the survey. The mental health section included twelve special investigators and three supervisors in official capacity. In addition, several doctors and trainees worked for the mental health survey on a voluntary basis. The investigators, who were selected through the good offices of a Field Research Organisation specialising in opinion surveys, had considerable experience in field work. Both regular and voluntary supervisors were doctors in training for specialist degree in psychiatry, psychologists and social workers. Fortunately, a sense of enthusiasm and cohesion and a dedicated research orientation could be created which mitigated against slipshod work or casual recording of data that often vitiate field surveys.

THE AIMS OF THE STUDY

In keeping with the aims of the general health survey, the aims of the mental health survey were to determine the extent and volume of mental health problems and help planners to provide improved service facilities.

The specific aims were to find confirmation of the generally held premises that (*a*) poverty and urban stresses were causing extensive mental health problems in Calcutta, and (*b*) the number of chronically ill persons in the community at large must be high, because there are no large mental hospitals in the state.

There were also subsidiary aims:

1. To demarcate the vulnerable groups in terms of such demographic and ecological correlates as age, sex, economic groups, occupation, social status, marital status, family types and location of residence in Calcutta and its suburbs.
2. To determine stresses and strains on the families arising out of circumstantial pressures.
3. To delineate stresses on different ethnic groups and migrants.
4. To study help-seeking attitudes of the residents and their perception of the 'need' for help.

THE FIELD WORK

The primary team included one doctor from the health survey section, one investigator from the socio-economic section and one investigator from the mental health section. Each of the sections had their own supervisors. All the members of the team visited the households together, with priority being given to the health examination. On the first day details about the family structure as well as demographic information were recorded, the main mental health schedules were completed the following day, so as not to take up too much time of the respondents and to avoid fatigue. Two or three subsequent visits were made to interview the people who were left out at the time of the initial interviews. Where families had moved out, or members could not be contacted or refused to cooperate, substitute families were interviewed according to a formula of sampling. Hence, the total number of families remained the same as during the first stage sampling.

The field work was completed in nearly eight months (excluding six weeks of training, two weeks of trials on the field and another four weeks of isolated checks of suspected cases and stray 'mopping-up'). The difficulties faced by the mental health investigators while interviewing people were not very great. On the whole respondents were cooperative, the Bengali speaking majority, the core group, was happy to be given an opportunity to talk about their problems. Suspiciousness, hostility and anti-government attitudes were certainly seen, but these were isolated phenomena. The presence of a doctor as well as the health examination were of immense help, but the expertise of the investigators and the fact that they were women were instrumental in obtaining the cooperation of the respondents.

The supervisors acted as co-ordinators to maintain uniformity of reporting. They checked and verified the cases and scrutinised the schedules submitted by the investigators.

Investigators went in pairs to different areas and these pairings were frequently changed so as to rule out inter-investigator variability. The same household was visited at different times—early morning for interviewing the working members and late afternoon for interviewing housewives. Most households were visited twice or even thrice and cooperation and candour improved with repeated visits.

The 'head of the family', usually a male member, acted as the informant for the 'Family Report', but often his wife or other senior family members gave the information. Probable suppression of information was seldom suspected.

The Project Director frequently visited the field and personally supervised the data collection. On the whole the field work was characterised by a high degree of authenticity and uniformity.

TRAINING FOR THE TEAM

Extensive discussions were held with the supervisors to enable them to grasp the broad social aspects of the survey. They were particularly instructed not to make on the spot diagnoses or to proffer technical terms to the investigators. Their function was to guide the investigators, check on the accuracy of reporting and confirm the broad categories.

As stated earlier, the investigators had previous experience in field work. They were given six weeks of intensive training in the behavioural aspects of the broad psychiatric categories. They met psychiatric patients whom they interviewed in the presence of qualified psychiatrists in the OPD. Care was taken to impress on them that they were only to record answers, observations and problems objectively, though sympathetically. During the six weeks of training, they practised administering the questionnaire to neurotic patients and their relatives, and later administered the questionnaire in the field before the commencement of actual work. A handbook was prepared on the method of administering the schedules and the investigators were asked to familiarise themselves with it.

THE SURVEY METHOD

The method used was the 'Household Survey Questionnaire and Interview' method. The title and the rationale behind the procedure are quoted here from Murphy (1982).

Assistants ask a series of precisely worded questions and bring back the answers with or without their own comments, and submit the results to psychiatrists for the latter to assess and classify . . . . Its main advantage is that within a given research budget one can, with such lesser trained interviewers [non-medical], cover a larger population and/or take time to enquire about lesser levels of mental distress than would normally be brought to the attention of any medical practitioner. Where subjects answer truthfully, therefore, one can frequently get a subjective picture of their disorders which is unlikely to be got in any other way from such a population, although there may still be a problem of assessing how this subjective picture relates to psychiatric classifications employed in the same, or more importantly in another, society.

The most notable surveys in which this method has been used are the Midtown Manhattan (Srole *et al.*, 1962) and the Stirling County (Leighton *et al.*, 1963b) surveys.

Though the Kota study (Carstairs and Kapur, 1976) also used this method, it adopted a specially constructed schedule: the 'Indian Psychiatric Survey Schedule' (Kapur *et al.*, 1974), which is a standardised instrument developed for psychiatric field work in Indian conditions. To our regret we found that this schedule was unsuitable for our study. This schedule, used by non-medical investigators, endeavours to elicit the gamut of psychiatric symptoms which are also interpreted by these investigators. Suspected cases are referred to an experienced psychiatrist who has to conduct a detailed examination of the subject. Informants are also asked questions about 'symptoms' in other members of the family. However, at the end of these lengthy exercises diagnoses or disability ratings are not made. The Kota study uses the IPSS and gives broad groupings, like psychoses or depression. Though these are not meant to be diagnoses, but they can be used as such, with some misgivings. The authors have discussed the unsatisfactory nature of disease classification, but most of the symptoms elicited by the IPSS are those which are elaborated as patterns of disease in psychiatric textbooks. This questionnaire is not a symptom checklist and it is not clear what other significance these symptoms may have. Varieties of sleep disturbances (26 items on somatic symptoms are included in the IPSS), are studied but these are meant only to show 'sleeplessness' and 'somatic symptoms'. Also, for a population survey schedule, it accords little importance to mental retardation (one question to a relative) and epilepsy (one question to the subject, with elaboration to be sought if he reports positively). Finally, the scoring defies common sense. *Any one* (or more) of the symptoms, whether terrifying dreams, or poor appetite, or hallucinations can make a 'case'. Other studies which do not make diagnoses usually ascertain the degrees of disability or differentiate between major and minor illnesses. Since the IPSS does not have such provisions, arbitrary groupings have to be made for correlation with other factors such as demography and social dysfunction. Adding up of symptoms for such groupings, as done in the Kota study, seems rather illogical since the symptoms elicited are often of disparate dimensions.

The Indian Psychiatric Interview Schedule—IPIS (on which the Survey Schedule—IPSS—is based) may be useful in studying symptom patterns or psychopathology in Indian patients, but its conversion into a survey schedule by adding the informant section, does not seem to have been very successful.

THE SAMPLING PROCEDURE

The sampling was done by the Indian Statistical Institute using the two-stage stratified technique. The stratification was on an economic basis. All the 120 census blocks of the 1971 Census of Calcutta, and 8 villages in the Metropolitan Development Area were under purview of the design. At the first stage, a set included 20 households in each sample block or village giving different weightage to various groups of households on the basis of monthly per capita household expenditure. These sets of 20 households were randomly selected, 8 each from the lower and middle per capita expenditure groups and 4 from the upper group. At the second stage, the expenditures of the selected households were verified and, if necessary, the groupings were readjusted.

The word 'household' was loosely used. Many people who did not live in proper houses, for example, pavement dwellers, were also included. For homeless people, a nearby shop or a vacant lot served to provide the 'address'. Institutions, such as hostels or homes (orphanages), were counted as 'unitary households'.

Sampling in community surveys is often faulty because institutions and 'transients' are not taken into account (Gruenberg, 1965). In the present survey, however, the first category was taken care of as mentioned earlier. But the issue of 'transients' (usually circulating grandparents or married daughters visiting parents) proved to be a different problem. Many families in Calcutta have their roots in villages not far from the city. Family members often interchange residences between the village home and the city house (*bari* and *basa* in the local dialect), or some of them live in one place and the rest live in the other. The socio-economic schedule for the survey classified the family members as 'usual members', that is, those who ate meals 30 days in a month together, and others as 'casual members'. Only the 'usuals' were considered to constitute the total number of family members. The monthly expenditure of the family (only 'usual' members) was obtained by adding the expenditure on items, such as,food, clothing and entertainment, for the entire month, dividing this figure by the number of the family members yielded the per capita expenditure. The economic stratification was done on the basis of this expenditure.

The sample lists provided the name of the 'head of the family', address, number of family members and the approximate expenditure per month per family. All these items were checked, corrected or modified whenever necessary.

There were three 'substitute lists'. If a sampled family had moved out, the next exact substitute was taken. However, if that family could not be located either, the second substitute was used. As a result, no sample families were left out.

THE INTERVIEW SCHEDULES

Two schedules were developed for structured interviews (see Appendices):

1. The Family Schedule—for interviewing the 'head of the family', who answered for other members.
2. The Individual Schedule—for interviewing all adult individuals. It was administered as a verbal self-report questionnaire.

The Family Schedule/Family Report

The informants answered each question either in affirmative or in negative for each member of the family. After completion of the set, elaborations were sought for the positive answers. The questions were non-technical, easy to understand and unambiguous. Indigenous terms for certain well known abnormalities were incorporated as additional explanations.

There were five sections in the Family Schedule:

1. The section relating to demographic and other aspects was in the form of a chart. Therefore, comparative position regarding most items, for example, education, could be seen at a glance for all the family members.
2. Children's section—the first half of this section included questions on developmental and early childhood problems of all the family members.

   The second half dealt with usual behaviour problems of children only. Parents had to answer several questions on mental retardation, in addition to identifying the retarded.
3. Adult's section—several insignificant items of information

including positive achievements of the family were sought through the questions, in order to eliminate suspicion and establish rapport. The emphasis of the target questions was on behavioural aspects. There were 6 questions on 'abnormal types' and another 6 on 'abnormal behaviour'. These 'abnormality patterns' were influenced by a study by Bhattacharya (1986), which enquired into the common Bengali perceptions of mental illness. These were very similar to those described by the relatives of a patient taken to the OPD.

The question whether there was any (one or more) person with mental illness in the family was asked separately.

4. In case of any mental illness, treatment undertaken, type of help sought, desired, or preferred were recorded in this section.
5. This section contained questions on performance of puja, rituals, maintenance of pollution rules, on dissensions within the family as well as between the family and its neighbours.

Many questions were asked, but no attempts were made to obtain stringent verification of these matters.

'Informant interview' is often criticised, mainly because so much depends on the veracity and perceptiveness of the informant. Regarding the first point, nothing specific could be done apart from establishing good rapport; the second problem was overcome by recording details of behaviour as well as identification. 'With such informants one can only reliably enquire into behaviour, not sensations; signs, not symptoms in the conventional modern sense' (Murphy, 1982).

The Individual Report Schedule/IRS

As stated earlier, we accepted that apart from people with gross behavioural problems, there would be others with psychological complaints of the kind that psychiatrists commonly diagnose as neuroses. By examining the history sheets of 500 patients diagnosed at our institute as one type of neurosis or other, the most common types of complaints were selected and incorporated into a questionnaire. This was administered to psychiatric patients, general hospital outpatients as well as the accompanying relatives. After several modifications, a set of 13 questions was finally selected. The emphasis was on easy understandability and acceptance of the questions by the non-patient (or non-complaining) population, because the vast majority was expected to be composed of such people. In addition to the above, there were six questions on somatic complaints and one on sleep (with two subsidiary ones on it).

Complaints relating to sex problems are not common in our OPDs, and ordinary people are likely to be offended if they are questioned about them openly. Hence, items pertaining to sexual difficulty were not included in this survey, in contrast to the Kota study (Carstairs and Kapur, 1976) where these were prominent. Complaints regarding menstrual problems are very common, but these were not considered to have many psychological implications, over and above those conveyed by general somatisation.

The answers were recorded as positive or negative, and confirmation of the fact that these were not random answers was sought by asking questions about the duration of the complaints. If the subject hesitated or was very vague about the time since he/she had first noticed the problem, then the instruction was to record 'no'. Though not much importance was attached to the duration of the complaints, yet a very long duration ('years' or 'since childhood') suggested personality traits. All the questions were related to recent complaints, but no answer was time-barred, provided the problem was still present. On the other hand any problem that had occurred previously, but was not present at the time of the inquiry was not recorded. After the schedule was completed, subjects were asked to elaborate, both as to the type of complaints and their probable reasons, which were recorded in detail. Physical illnesses, both past and present, were recorded in this 'free comments' section.

In the Family Report, we started by asking about the positive features of the family; in the Individual Report the starting point was recreation and leisure. These questions not only helped to establish rapport but also helped to gauge the severity of the complaints to some extent.

Though the tools used in the study had all the fallacies which one comes across in the construction of questionnaires, yet they did have some measure of reliability and validity (see appendices). We would like to designate the persons identified in the field as 'potential cases'. Goldberg (1972), while quoting another author, and disapproving of 'complaints inventories', maintains that they merely represent a 'tabulation of misery' . . . 'especially true for individuals of low social class, since miseries and dissatisfaction are universally found in people of low status in industrial societies'. However, since most authors find neuroses to be 'significantly higher in low social groups' as well, it should not be deemed illogical to associate complaints with neuroses. The real issue is the concept underlying neurosis as a 'disease', one of the most controversial subjects in psychiatry.

The Interviews

Investigators with previous experience in 'opinion survey' type of work were aware of the risk of asking 'leading questions' and were skilled enough not to influence the subjects in answering one way or another. They were trained to administer the schedules to normals and cases under supervision in out-patient departments. Variability between investigators was found; this was sought to be eliminated by rotating them areawise and forming several pairs. Since they were merely recording and not rating or interpreting, the problem of variability remained in the area of establishing rapport or writing adequate explanatory notes. This problem did not affect the work to any great extent.

Other common difficulties with questionnaires, such as 'response style', or tendency to give 'good' or 'expected' answers, could not be avoided altogether. Non-Bengali workers had a tendency to say 'no' for everything! But we were aware of the problem, and judicious leading questions had to put in such cases.

Each investigator carried a master sheet of the questionnaire in Bengali and Hindi, but the schedules were marked in English. These were later coded for computer use. The questions were in the patients' usual language, with several alternative terms. We were not translating symptoms, but attempting just the obverse, as happens in clinical practice. Patients complain in their own language, psychiatrists interpret and record these in their professional language (or jargon). It so happened that our department followed the practice of recording the patients' complaints verbatim. We did not, therefore, face the problem of literal or conceptual translations. The investigators were all Bengalis and could converse in English. Some of them were also proficient in Hindi. The non-Bengali segment of the sample spoke at least one of these three languages.

CODING

The *coding* was done directly and not by a computer. The supervisors scrutinised each schedule thoroughly, checked them several times for correction of entries and initial coding. Final diagnóstic coding was done by the Consultant (the author). Each set of schedule was thoroughly read; positive and negative answers were assessed after taking into account comments by the relatives, investigators and supervisors, as well as non-quantifiable information like achievements and leisure activities. The assessments were further evaluated against the demographic background of the respondents and only then the codings were finalised.

Some 'diagnoses' or categorisation followed the criteria set earlier, but for others informants assertions were relied upon.

Repeated scrutiny was also done at the final stage and these manually verified and coded schedules were then analysed by the computer.

CATEGORIES OR 'DIAGNOSES'

The following rather loosely formulated criteria were adopted to designate categories, based on the Family Report given by informants.

Psychoses

1. The presence of at least 2 items (out of 7) of the sub-section on 'unusual behaviour'.
2. Loss of work/disruption of studies/marked reduction or absence of expected activities.
3. Identification by the informant as mentally ill (vernacular— *matha-kharap, pagol*).
4. Confirmatory notes/comments.

Abnormal Personality/(?)Psychoses

1. The presence of at least 4 items (out of 9) of the sub-section on 'abnormal personality'.

2. And/or presence of identification as 'extremely suspicious' (vernacular—*sandeho-batik*).
3. Employed/earning something/disruption or reduction in habitual activities nil or minor.
4. The absence of identification as mentally ill.

Mental Retardation

Severe Mental Retardation (SMR)—The presence of all the following criteria: delayed milestones, inability to understand, or learn, or look after self; suggestive appearance; identification by the informant (preferably parents) as 'retarded' (vernacular— *jara-budhi, haba-goba*).

Mild Mental Retardation (MMR)—The presence of much lower school or learning achievements compared to siblings or other children of the same age group which required to be confirmed by informants (parents) as not due to naughtiness or physical illness; or lack of initiative (or opportunities) on the part of the parents.

In addition, identification as 'dull', or the presence of one or more symptoms as in the 'severe' category (vernacular—*boka*).

Epilepsy

The presence of epilepsy—identification by the informant (preferably parents) as suffering from 'fits' or *mrigyi* and suggestive description of the fits from an eye witness.

In the case of adults, additional confirmation was sought that these were not functional fits (hysteria), or unconsciousness due to physical illnesses.

Further confirmatory evidence was the treatment being given.

Conditions Identified by Indigenous Concepts—
Senile Loss of Memory, Possession State and 'Purity Mania'

1. Identification by vernacular equivalents—*bhimroti, thakur-bhar*

and *suchi-bai*. (The English equivalents are those given above respectively).

2. Elaborative examples as confirmatory evidence.

Psychoneuroses

Emphasis was laid on somatic complaints, as it is well-known that these often actually denote psychological problems. In the Individual Report, similar complaints were grouped together to indicate subtypes of neuroses, but these are not to be considered definite categories. The grouping was considered necessary to distinguish hysteria and obsessional states from other neuroses.

CRITERIA

1. At least three complaints of anxiety or depression type; sleep disturbance; at least 2 items of somatic complaints (out of 6).
2. Definitive comments on the onset by the subject, or history of some major event in the family immediately prior to onset.

Obsessional States and Phobias

One or two classical symptoms with at least two other complaints. If identified as *suchi-bai* then the person's own confirmation had to be sought.

Hysteria

Only hysterical fits were inquired into 'Fits' or 'unconsciousness' admitted by the subjects, lasting for more than a few minutes, absence of epilepsy (or *mrigyi*) in the Family Report. Occurrences were required to be frequent.

3

Findings of the Survey— Rates

BASIC DEMOGRAPHIC DATA OF THE SAMPLE

Number of sampled families—2512
Number of sampled persons—13,335

IN the initial analysis the sample consisted of 14,308 persons, however, 973 persons were later excluded because they did not fulfil the criterion of 'usual members' of the families.

During the period between sampling and the actual survey 85 persons in the total sample had died. Since these dead persons were in the family structure available to us, they were included in the Family Reports for the purpose of detecting suicides.

Distribution of Sampled Persons by

Sex

Males	7235	54.2 per cent
Females	6100	45.7 per cent

Marital Status (Adults of Age 14 years and Above)

	Males	Per cent	Females	Per cent
Single	2025	39.9	1017	25.2
Married	2957	58.3	2462	61.1
Widow/Widowers/Others	90	1.7	550	13.6
	5072	99.9	4029	99.9

(Others: Divorced or separated, grouped together with widows, etc., because the number was small.)

Location (Areas Under the Mental Health Survey)

		Per cent
Calcutta Proper (Area with Calcutta Postal Codes)	6567	49.2
Calcutta Slums	831	6.2
Outside Calcutta (Areas Outside Calcutta 'Proper')	5010	37.5
Outside Villages	927	6.9
	13335	99.8

(Calcutta including the area surrounding it, under the jurisdiction of the Calcutta Metropolitan Development Authority, has a radius of approximately 50 miles. The surrounding area is economically linked with Calcutta and is considered urban though it includes agricultural land and villages, besides small towns and suburbs of Calcutta.)

Age: Children

		Per cent	Per cent
0–13 years	4234	31.75	31.75

Age: Adults

		Per cent	Per cent
14–24 years	3049	22.86	
25–39 years	2986	22.39	
40–49 years	1371	10.28	
50–59 years	909	6.81	
60+ years	786	5.89	68.23
			99.98

Education (Adults)

			Per cent
Illiterate to Elementary	Low	2766	30.39
Primary to High School	Middle	3848	42.28
Matriculation and Above	High	2487	27.33

Occupation and Occupational Status Groups

		(Sample Adults)	Per cent
High	Professional, Executive, Businessman, Clerk, Teacher, Nurse, Technician, Shopowner, Hotel-keeper, Caretaker, Farmer (Owning Land), Railway Driver, etc.	3743	41.13
Middle	Peon, Bearer, Shop Assistant, Barber,	3505	38.51

	(Sample Adults)	Per cent
Low	Fisherman, Gardener, Dairyman, Tailor, Skilled Worker, Driver Vendor, Cook, Waiter, Servant, Sweeper, Washerman, Cobbler, Rickshaw/Cart Puller, Labourer (Daily Wage), Miscellaneous Low Earning Occupations (Beggar, Prostitute, etc.)	1853	20.36
	9101	100

The division is made on the basis of social status of these occupations. Unemployed persons, housewives and students were placed in the status group of the highest ranking person in the family. For example, a teacher in the family will be assigned high status ignoring the occupati   of the other members, including that of the head, who may be a worker.

Type of Family

	Nuclear	Extended	Joint	Unitary	Total
Number of Persons	4426	1806	6740	363	13335
Percentage	33.2	13.5	50.5	2.7	= 99.9
Number of Families	981	297	871	363	2512
Percentage	39.1	11.8	34.7	14.4	= 100

Definitions of Family Types

Nuclear	Single earning member (or husband and wife) living with wife and children.
Extended	Above, with one or more non-earning adults or dependent members living together.
Joint	Two adult earning members (other than husband and wife) sharing family expenses (irrespective of other dependent adults).
Unitary	A single person living on his or her own or in an institution.

Religion

		Per cent
Hindu	11925	89.43
Muslim	1050	7.87
Christian	155	1.16
Others	205	1.54
	13335	100

Per Capita Expenditure Groups

(Obtained from the total sample of the Survey, CMDA Report.) The monthly expenditure of each family was divided by the number of family members to determine the per capita expenditure. Given below is the grouping of families according to this figure.

Per Capita Expenditure	Population Distribution (Per cent of Population)	Average Family Size
Rs. 0 to 55	20	6.2
Rs. 56 to 136	60	4.7
Rs. 137 and above	20	3.7

Economic Strata of the Mental Health Survey Sample

		Per cent
Low	2697	20.2
Middle	7940	59.5
High	2698	20.2
	13335	99.9

Linguistic or Ethnic Groups

		Per cent
Bengali	9493	71.19
Non-Bengali	3842	28.81
	13335	100

PREVALENCE OF DISORDERS IN THE POPULATION

Estimated Number of Affected Persons and Rate per Thousand

Two sets of prevalence figures have been given, one is based on estimates of cases and the other on the actual cases found. The estimates were obtained by using raising factors or 'multipliers' appropriate to the sampling design.

While it is common to find one person suffering from two different physical diseases at the same time (for example, tuberculosis and blindness), this is unusual in psychiatric diagnosis. The Ninth Revision of the International Classification of Diseases (WHO, 1978a) recommends psychiatric diagnoses to be made as the main and subsidiary diagnosis. In calculating the rates of disorder in the estimated population we have assigned only the main diagnosis to each affected person.

Multiple diagnoses, however, were taken into account in computing the rates of disorder in the sample population. These differences in computation have led to certain discrepancies in the rate per thousand, between Tables 3.1 and 3.2. The listing of categories in the tables are in order of importance, that is, from the most important to the least important.

TABLE 3.1
Estimated Number of Persons Under Broad Categories of Disorders

Severe Retardation	45,000
Psychoses	72,400
Epilepsy	62,800
Mild Retardation	132,000
Severe Personality Disorder	98,800
Psychoneuroses	858,000
Possession State and 'Purity Mania'	161,000
	1,430,000

Total of Estimated Rates of the above Disorders—138.4 per 1000 of Population

TABLE 3.2
Rates Obtained from the Sample Population
(N = 13335)

	Number of Cases	Rate per 1000	After Age Adjustments
Severe Retardation	51	3.8	4.1
Psychoses	68	5.0	4.4
Epilepsy	79	5.9	6.0
Mild Retardation	149	11.1	12.4
Severe Personality Disorder	110	8.2	7.2
Psychoneuroses	998	74.8	64.9
	1,455	108.8	99.9
Possession State and *Suchi-bai*	204	15.2	
Memory Disorders	67	5.2	
	1,726	129.2	

MORBIDITY ESTIMATES

Estimated number of people under the survey—10,326,000.

The other table (Table 3.2) shows the rates calculated from the sample population, as well as the rates after age adjustment. The age adjusted rates are different from the crude rates, depending on whether the conditions are present in all age groups or not. While discussing the results, only the rates obtained from the sample have been used for the purpose of comparison with other Indian studies.

The rates of disorders in different universes are presented in Tables 3.3a and 3.3b. Some of the disorders given here have not been included in the morbidity list.

DETAILED ANALYSIS OF THE SAMPLE

TABLE 3.3a
Prevalence of Disorders as Obtained from the Family Report

Mental Retardation	*Number*	*Per cent of Total Sample* (N = 13,335)
Severe Retardation	51	0.38
Mild Retardation	149	1.11
	200	1.49

Children	*Number*	*Per cent of Child Sample* (N = 4234)
Severe Retardation	26	0.61
Mild Retardation	81	1.91
	107	2.52

Multiple Defects with Mental Retardation	*Number*	*Per cent of MR* (N = 200)
Persence of Conduct Disorder with Mental Retardation	25	12.5
Presence of Physical Defects with Mental Retardation	28	14.0
Presence of Epilepsy with Mental Retardation	12	6.0

Table 3.3a (Contd.)

Epilepsy	Number	
Children	27	0.63 per cent of Child Sample (N = 4234)
Adults	52	0.57 per cent of Adult Sample (N = 9101)
	79	0.59 per cent of Total Sample (N = 13,335)

Adults	Number	Per cent of Adult Sample (N = 9101)
Severe Retardation	25	0.27
Mild Retardation	68	0.74
	93	1.01

Educational Backwardness	Number	Per cent of Literate Population
Persons Who did not do Well in School Due to Naughtiness/Forgetfulness/Dullness/Restlessness	442	5.5

Conduct Disorder in Children	Number	Per cent (N = 4234)
Complaints of Parents: Very Naughty (317)/Would Not Study (286)/ Runs Away from Home and School (82)/ Fights and Quarrels (124) Out of These Totals		
Severity was Reached by	106	2.5
Stammering in Children	86	2.03

TABLE 3.3b
Problems and Disorders in Adults as Obtained by the Family Report

	Number	Rate/1000 (N = 9101)
Persons who were in a disturbed psychotic state	23	2.5
Persons who were in an active psychotic state, but quiet and manageable	31	3.4
Persons who were in an active psychotic state, but were depressed	14	1.5
	68	7.4

Table 3.3b (Contd.)

	Number	*Rate/1000* *(N = 9101)*
Persons who were considered highly abnormal with unusual behaviour but not considered psychotic by their relatives (usually employed or performed house work)	73	8.0
Persons who were extremely suspicious (*Sandeho-batik*—vernacular for such behaviour)	37	4.0
	110	12.0
Total Psychoses and Related Disorders	178	19.5
Persons with compulsive behaviour regarding pollution (*Suchi-bai*—vernacular)	162	17.8
Persons who had possession state (*Thakur-bhar*—vernacular)	42	4.6
Persons over the age of 60 years who had memory disturbances and associated problems (*Bhimroti*—vernacular)	67	7.3
Persons who consumed alcohol (whether amounting to alcoholism or not)	283	31.09
Persons who had *ganja* or opium habit	53	5.8
Persons, usually young adults, described as anti-social and who had been in jail or police custody	30	3.2
Persons with conduct disorders of delinquency type	22	2.4
Persons who left home or became *sadhus*	9	0.98
Number of suicides in the families visited	19	2.08
Persons who were considered highly irritable, but otherwise normal	141	15.4

TABLE 3.4
Neurotic Disorders as Obtained by the Individual Report
(N = 9101)

Somatic Symptoms	*Number*	*Rate/1000*
Major (4–5 Complaints)	1226	134.7
Minor (2–3 Complaints)	1237	135.9
Sleep Disturbance	1302	143.0
Number of Persons with		
Functional Fits and Faints	179	

Table 3.4 (Contd.)

Somatic Symptoms	Number	Rate/1000
Possibly Hysteria	54	5.9
Predominant Anxiety Symptoms	1141	
Possibly Severe Anxiety State	95	10.4
Anxiety State	167	18.3
Obsessional and Phobic Symptoms	487	
Possibly Obsessional States	78	8.5
Phobic States	32	3.5
Depressive Symptoms	668	
Possibly Depressive Neurosis	363	39.8
Multiplicity of Neurotic Symptoms	209	
Pan-Neurosis	209	22.9
Total Neurotic Disorders	998	109.6

(Possession State and *suchi-bai* were not included since these were not detected by the Individual Report.)

DISCUSSION ON THE CATEGORIES OR 'DIAGNOSIS'

Active Psychoses/Abnormal Personality/Paranoid States

In formulating the above named categories set criteria were followed. However, the condition termed 'abnormal personality' was not anticipated when planning the survey, since such cases neither visit doctors nor attend hospitals. The appropriate criteria for this condition were decided after examining the trial schedules. Active psychoses included schizophrenia and manic-depressive psychosis, but no attempts were made to identify it. The 'cases' detected were all 'chronic' cases, some of whom had undergone treatment or were attending hospitals or seeing private psychiatrists. Diagnosis of chronic cases is difficult even at clinics in Calcutta, because the majority manifest mixed symptoms of schizo-affective nature. However, in designating a case as 'depression' we relied on the history, complaints, treatment being received and previous psychiatric assessments.

The division of psychoses into behavioural categories, such as, 'disturbed', 'quiet' and 'depressed' was done entirely for the practical purpose of ascertaining the number of disordered persons requiring hospitalisation. It was thought that the 'disturbed' and the 'depressed' cases would indicate the extent of this need. However, this was not fully realised. There were very few cases of depression (1.5/1000 adult population), raising the doubt that many such cases may have been missed. It is certainly possible that some cases may have been confused with 'quiet' psychosis and others with depressive neurosis. Psychotic depression seen in Calcutta is usually not the retarded, delusional, chronic or resistant type described in textbooks. Most cases manifested symptoms of anxiety, obsessive-phobic or hypochondriacal neurosis. Hysterical demands for sympathy and attention often mask depressive moods. Such cases might have been confused with other categories.

'Abnormal personality' and paranoid states have been categorised separately at times but more often they are referred to as 'related disorders', as these are considered 'active' conditions at par with psychoses.

'Abnormal personality' (inclusive of (?)psychosis and paranoid states) consisted of a variety of abnormal behaviour, the main characteristic being aggressive violence for men and the same manifested in a different way, i.e., shouting and abusing, in the case of women. Other oddities of behaviour were also invariably present.

These persons were not considered to be mentally ill, but besides aggressiveness, their behaviour suggested gross departure from the usual. Since many of them were earning members, their families may have been motivated not to label them as ill. Some of them were curt, rude, or refused to talk to the investigators; but the majority who were interviewed, appeared to be 'normal' to the supervisors. They showed no overt psychotic symptoms. Evasive answers and denials were more common in the paranoid cases, but additional illustrative comments (e.g., 'keeping doors and windows always locked') and labelling were seen in these cases.

Care was taken to distinguish psychotics and abnormal personalities from people who showed excessive irritability. Such people shouted, abused and broke things at the slightest provocation, but they could be easily pacified and were apologetic later.

The history of past mental illness in the family was carefully elicited; it was also ascertained that the affected person had completely recovered. The rate of 'past illness' has not been included in the overall rates, but it was important to obtain the history so as to make sure that only chronic and active cases were included.

Mental Retardation

Severe cases were easily identified and all the criteria for diagnosis could be satisfied. The mild type signified gross discrepancies between age and school or other achievements, or the type of simple tasks the child or the adolescent could perform. Even an illiterate mother could always point out the child who was dull or slower as compared to the other children. However, when the mother was incapable of giving such information, other people had to be depended on for this information. It is likely that the moderately retarded group was distributed between the other two groups, but the likelihood of this group being clubbed with the mild types is stronger. (For further discussion see the section on retardation.)

Epilepsy

Major (grand mal) types were not difficult to detect, but minor types (petit mal) or atypical cases may not have been reported. It is unlikely that epilepsy and hysteria were confused, because the latter required other confirmation. The diagnosis of epilepsy was supported by the drug treatment that many of the patients were receiving.

Educational Backwardness, Delayed Milestones

These were enquired for all persons in the sample. The first category particularly indicates poor school records. Some mild cases of mental retardation were also included in this category, provided they had some schooling. A majority of the cases with delayed development were mentally retarded.

Conduct Disorder in Children

This category is indicative of parents' evaluation of children being 'very naughty' which, admittedly, is a relative concept. Destructiveness and disobedience added some weight, but the primary factor in categorising these children was their being different from other children. This estimate is very low, because details regarding lying, stealing, or bed-wetting were neither asked for nor volunteered by the parents. Details regarding withdrawal, timidity or shyness were sought, but parents did not report these.

Anti-social Activities

An indirect question was asked to elicit information about anti-social activities. The respondents were asked if there was any political worker in the family and whether anyone had been convicted and for what reasons. The answers obtained indicate 140 political workers (i.e., 1.5 per cent of the adult sample), and of these 112 had got into trouble with the law. Of these, 75 had been convicted for pre- and post-independence political activities, land and property disputes, and 30 for criminal offences. No reasons were given in the remaining seven cases. Delinquent behaviour and anti-social activities, whether in conflict with the law or not, were reported in the case of young adult males. Political association was not seen in these cases.

Persons Who Disappeared or Became Sadhus

It is well known among psychiatrists in India that people in this category are often mentally ill, or at least potentially so (Mayer-Gross *et al.*, 1958). Information regarding this was taken into account in characterising 'pathological families', i.e., where one and the same family reported such cases, or where there was more than one person suffering from mental disorder, anti-social activity by a family member, alcoholism, and where unexplained tension and quarrels existed. For example, one family had one psychotic (in a mental hospital), one 'abnormal personality', and four unmarried brothers and sisters who lived together but never spoke to each other. There were 56 such families (2.2 per cent of the total number of families). Loss of potential cases through disappearance, etc., was found to be negligible.

Alcohol and Drugs

No attempts were made to ascertain the type of drinking. Hence some upper class social drinkers are included here who were probably not addicts. The majority of heavy drinkers were sweepers and factory workers, who readily admitted their habit. A common complaint in slum areas was ill-treatment by alcoholic husbands.

It was observed that many of those who either consumed alcohol or consumed both alcohol and drugs had other problems, such as, 'abnormal personality' or excessive irritability. Abuse of such drugs as *ganja* (*Cannabis indica*), opium and pethidine was reported. On the whole, problems related to drugs and alcohol were briefly covered in this survey.

Memory Disturbances

The identification of cases of dementia was easy as an indigenous concept of senility exists in Bengali culture—*bhimroti* which implies both loss of memory and childish or incongruous behaviour. However, severity of the disability could not be ascertained.

Suicide

Information regarding death in the family due to accident or suicide was obtained. However, no further details were obtained.

Psychoneuroses

Diagnosis of psychoneuroses was made only where neurotic symptoms were of some severity as judged by sleep disturbances. Though anxiety and depressive types of complaints were common, many individuals gave mixed responses of different types which made sub-classification difficult. However, this was still attempted to ascertain the nature of the complaints.

Anxiety and Depression

Affect or feeling of anxiety was found to be pervasive. The highest number of positive responses for an individual item in the self-report was for 'worrying too much' (1513), followed by an item in the self-report (IRS) for phobia—unfounded and 'intense fear of anything, (1488). The other items related to anxiety were 'feeling of nervousness, (1345), and 'tension and restlessness' (1055). Large number of responses were also obtained for two items related to depression—'feelings of helplessness' (833), and 'loss of interest' (715). Only 20 per cent of the affected persons complaining of several anxiety symptoms were classified under 'anxiety state', whereas over 50 per cent of those manifesting depressive symptoms were categorised as 'depression'. The reason being that when the symptoms were mixed, depressive symptoms were given priority. A majority of the people believed that their condition was due to adverse circumstances, usually acute financial distress. Illnesses and unemployment were also frequently cited as the possible reasons. Economic dependency on others was a potent source of complaint among elderly female relatives of the earning members. Many individuals did not give any explanation or causes for their feelings of depression. (Anxiety symptoms concomitant with physical illness were computed separately.)

Hysteria

Only hysterical fits were studied, and this perhaps accounted for the low rate. As other types of conversion symptoms are rarely seen even in psychiatric clinics in Calcutta, it is likely that not much of this category was missed.

Possession state is often perceived as a hysterical manifestation. However, as the status is uncertain, it has been classified as a 'related disorder'.

Obsessional States

The author had previously (Chakraborty and Banerji, 1975) tried to demonstrate that the culturally recognised condition of *suchi-bai* is similar to the clinically diagnosed condition of obsessive compulsive disorder. However, not all cases of *suchi-bai* identified by the informants have been categorised as obsessional state, because the diagnosis of neurotic conditions was based on the person's self-evaluation. If the person had no complaints or denied having a symptom, then no diagnosis could be made. *Suchi-bai* has, therefore, been shown here as a 'neurosis related disorder'.

Pan-Neurosis

Symptoms of a diverse nature with sleep disturbances and somatic complaints by one and the same person were found in many cases. For example, persons suffering from hysterical fits also manifested obsessional symptoms. Such individuals may have been typical 'yes-sayers' (people who say 'yes' to all questions). However, this pattern is not at all unusual among the OPD patients who are glad to talk about their problems spontaneously and structured questions are not asked.

Clinical patterns of neurotic symptoms were extensively and separately investigated in another study (see Addendum).

Neurotic Personality

To be placed in this category the symptoms had to persist for a very long time ('since childhood', 'always'). These cases also showed pan-neurosis. (This is not to be confused with 'abnormal personality' of the Family Report.)

Somatic Complaints

In computation somatic complaints were ignored if the person had any physical illness. It was observed that those who had numerous psychological problems also had several physical complaints. The most common complaint was related to 'weakness', followed by 'headache' and 'aches and pains'. (Detailed discussions are given in Chapter 5.)

Possession States and Purity Mania *(Suchi-bai)*

These two conditions are not included in any standard classification of psychiatric disorders. However, the first condition is found in many parts of the world. The second, though seen mostly in Bengali culture, is not an unusual phenomenon. It is very similar to obsessional neurosis, a common psychiatric disorder.

Possession state denotes possession of a person by a supernatural being (spirits, ghosts, the devil, gods or goddesses) which makes the possessed person behave abnormally. Some forms of these behaviour aberrations are socially approved and the person is revered whereas other forms are perceived to be indicative of 'madness' and the person is exorcised. Some authorities (Prince, 1968; Peters and Price-Williams, 1983) hold the view that the possession phenomena (or altered states of consciousness) are socially useful outlets for relieving tensions and should not be given a psychiatric label. Others (Langness, 1976) have argued that these states are forms of hysteria or even brief psychosis. Whatever way these phenomena are assessed, the fact is that they are no longer ignored in mental health surveys in Third World countries.

Possession states are found all over India. The early reported cases were presented as psychiatric disorders (Verma *et al.*, 1970; Teja *et al.*, 1970). Later field surveys have shown that the majority of cases never visited clinics (Venkataramaiah *et al.*, 1981; Chandrashekar, 1982; Chandrashekar *et al.*, 1982) and these authors are inclined to view possession states as non-pathological. We are in agreement with this viewpoint.

In Calcutta and its surrounding areas, possession by a deity, known as *thakur-bhar*, is well known. The possessed person behaves in a characteristic fashion, inspires respect and reverence and may even set up business as an oracle. In contrast, possession by an evil spirit (*bhut*) is rarely heard of nowadays. In the case of possession by *bhut*, the person's behaviour is not characteristic, though panic and fear are usually present. If this is reported at all, it is viewed either as a joke or as a falsehood. However, belief in ghosts is widespread and according to folklore, ghosts are said to cause 'temporary insanity'.

In the present survey only *thakur-bhar* or possession by a good spirit or deity was examined. We thought that if it was an open enquiry inclusive of questions on demons and ghosts, much of the seriousness of our purpose would have been lost. The answers would have been too unreliable and too varied to know what was being dealt with.

The Bengali term *suchi-bai* (purity mania) refers to a person who washes and cleans excessively in order to avoid pollution. It is recognised as an abnormality but the community has adopted a tolerant attitude towards it. It is viewed as a variation of the normal behaviour of elderly Brahmin widows (Chakraborty and Banerji, 1975). However, the affected person usually denies the symptom. For the purpose of this survey where a discrepancy existed between the informant's report and the person's self-report, the former was given credence, that is, the person was described as manifesting *suchi-bai* and not obsessional state.

The non-Bengali population was asked the same questions but the emphasis was not on the vernacular term.

DISCUSSION ON THE FINDINGS—PREVALENCE RATES

Taking only the most important and gross categories, the overall morbidity rate of nearly 109 per thousand population at risk is the highest in India.

Earlier only two studies had been conducted on a fairly large and properly sampled urban population, one by Verghese *et al.* (1973) at Vellore and the other by Sethi *et al.* (1974) at Lucknow. The overall rates were 66.2 and 67 per thousand population at Vellore and Lucknow respectively.

In addition to these, there is another study by Dube (1970) using a sample of urban and rural population around Agra, where a morbidity rate of 20 per thousand was found. A study by Shah and associates (1980) on a small urban sample at Ahmedabad gave a rate of 47 per thousand population.

The low but varying rates observed in rural studies in India are probably due to inadequate sampling; where sampling was methodical the rate was found to be very low, that is, 14.5 per thousand population (Mehta *et al.*, 1985).

Dube (1970) observed a low rate and little difference between the rural and industrial population. However, he did not attach much importance to neuroses (with the exception of hysteria) which may have led to biased results.

The high urban prevalence rates tend to support the hypothesis that urban environment leads to a high level of mental ill health. The rate in Calcutta being higher than that in other urban cities implicates its stressful living conditions and other complexities. Though Lucknow is a big city and a state capital it is not heavily industrialised, Vellore is a small town whereas industry has developed in Ahmedabad only in recent decades. None of these places can be compared to Calcutta as far as urban problems are concerned.

So far we have discussed only the overall rates. When some specific rates for adults are compared, interesting features emerge. Calcutta's high mental morbidity rate is mainly due to a high level of psycho-neuroses. The rate for gross psychoses in Calcutta (7.2/1000) is lower than that in Lucknow (20.4/1000), Ahmedabad (16.3/1000) or Vellore (9/1000). However, when 'psychosis related disorders' are added, the rate in Calcutta (19.4/1000) is almost the same as that in Lucknow.

One probable explanation for the low rate of gross psychoses in Calcutta could have been the exclusion of chronic cases from the field. It has been stated earlier that the stray population was covered by the survey. West Bengal does not have any large mental hospital, the nearest hospital is 500 miles away in the neighbouring state of Bihar. Certified cases from West Bengal have to wait for several months or even years before they can get admission there. The chronically disturbed people are kept in 'lunatic wards' in local jails. It was found that these cases along with 'vagrant lunatics' numbered around 5000 (the figure is an updated one from Chakraborty, 1972). Even if this figure was added to the estimates of 72,000 psychotics and nearly 100,000 related disorders, it would not affect the rates.

The differences in rates in the various surveys may be due to different methods or criteria adopted for diagnosis. The large difference in the Calcutta figures depended on whether a narrow or a wide set of criteria were used. The point to be noted is that the rates of psychoses found in Calcutta are well within the range found elsewhere in India.

It also appears that the *rate for chronic psychoses is low*; we expected a higher accumulation of such cases as facilities for custodial care are almost non-existent in the city. This low rate tends to support the hypothesis that psychoses in India are benign and the tendency towards chronicity is low. A probable explanation for this is the permissive and tolerant attitude of the Indian social milieu towards behavioural deviance. It is our surmise that some cases of persistent abnormal behaviour (termed 'abnormal personality') in this study were basically psychotic but laxity of societal codes prevented the development of psychosis.

Hence, it would appear that compared to the rural, urban population in India is more vulnerable to psychoses, but these psychoses tend to revert to normalcy or near normalcy because of a conducive social environment. It also seems that such conditions prevail in all urban centres irrespective of their complexities.

Urban complexities, however, seem to influence the development of psychoneuroses. It was observed that Calcutta differed significantly from all other places in India, with regard to these conditions.

The neuroses survey at Vellore (Verghese *et al.*, 1974) reported a rate of 47/1000 adults, while the rate in this study was 109.6/1000 adult population (excluding *suchi-bai* and possession states because of their doubtful status as neuroses). Neuroses rates in other parts of the country are even lower, 27 and 21 per thousand in Lucknow and Ahmedabad respectively. The possible reasons for the high rate of neuroses in Calcutta are many, one of it could be methodology.

The Vellore study used various tests for diagnoses, whereas the questionnaire method was used for the present study, and this could have given rise to the difference. This problem will be discussed in detail later; suffice it is to state here that though we claim our cases to be only potential ones, these indicate a high level of distress among a certain section of the Calcutta population, i.e., the Bengalis.

We believe that Bengalis in Calcutta and its suburbs are subjected to considerable stress, due to the prevailing conditions. Among the reasons given for their feelings of distress were adverse circumstances, unemployment, insecurity, poverty, illness, etc. The atmosphere in the city during the field work was ridden with anxiety. Failure to cope with this anxiety made it pathological.

The prevailing situation in Calcutta has to be seen in the perspective of the state's culture, history and economics. Bengali personality has to be taken into account because personality is shaped by cultural learning, apart from constitutional and other factors. The national stereotype of the Bengali is that he is intelligent and artistic, but emotional, lazy and 'soft' (as 'rice-eaters' are supposed to be). Bengal had always been a fertile, rainsodden land where the need to be tough so as to control the elements never arose. Industrial development (where heavy labour is done by migrants, Bengalis excel in skilled work, particularly electrical) notwithstanding, Bengalis remained largely preoccupied by cults, rituals, festivals and 'artistic' pursuits. In more recent decades, these were replaced to a great extent by ideological politics.

The partition of the state at the time of independence ruptured the Bengali social fabric. Millions of refugees poured in from East Pakistan (now Bangladesh) and remained unrehabilitated and unintegrated for many years. To this overstrained situation was added economic recessions in the entire eastern region of the country. Migration from rural areas and neighbouring states, which had been going on since Calcutta was founded 300 years ago, increased after partition to bring the population pressure to bursting point. At the same time, the educated upper classes began leaving the city for better prospects abroad. A deep change in the social structure followed.

The Bengali's reaction to these calamities is helpless anxiety, though externally only avoidance and apathy are manifested. As will be discussed later, it also seems that the sons of this mother-worshipping culture are increasingly dependent on their wives and mothers to solve their problems, which is leading to subtle changes in sex roles as well.

It is our contention that these social stresses together with the economic and urban conditions underlie the high rates of anxiety and depressive complaints observed in this study. Non-Bengalis living in Calcutta though subjected to some of these stresses, showed a lower rate of neuroses (19.3/1000 adult population) which is closer to the rates found elsewhere in India. The hypothesis regarding the influence of cultural factors is further strengthened by the observation of Verghese *et al.* (1974) who found no cases of obsessive compulsive neurosis in Vellore. The rates in Calcutta are 8.5/1000 for severe cases and 17.8 for the variant form—*suchi-bai*. Nandi *et al.* (1980) also observed a high rate for this condition as well as for other psychoneuroses in a selected group of Bengalis in Calcutta. Reasons for the high rates among Bengalis are high levels of anxiety on the one hand and the importance of rituals in Bengali life on the other (Chakraborty and Banerji, 1975). Rituals are an integral part of the psychopathology of obsessive compulsive disorder. How individual psychopathology finds expression through cultural rites, rituals and symbols has been discussed elsewhere (Chakraborty, 1974).

Underlying all forms of neuroses is anxiety, but it would appear that the expression of these forms is influenced by social attitudes or one may even say 'fashions'. Hysteria used to be a common form of neurosis but the gross conversion types have almost disappeared in the west and in India too this type is becoming rare. It is usually thought that hysteria is disappearing due to the spread of medical knowledge and education. On the whole, one agrees with this but there are other factors. The low rate reported in this study may be due to the fact that it is not a common condition, or because only one type of reaction was studied. Another reason could be the fairly frequent occurrences of possession state, which is also a dissociative trance like condition. The latter condition carries social approval and gives the 'possessed' a sense of power (Murphy, 1982), whereas conversion hysterias even with all the dramatic gestures fail to impress and are disapproved of. In hysteria the person abdicates the responsibility for the self and 'demands' care and attention, which the family, as the agent of a changed society, refuses to provide. In possession state on the other hand, the person 'aided' by supernatural agencies is more in a position to help, which he often does. However, we do not agree with the viewpoint that possession states should be considered pathological and at par with hysteria, which implies a derisive stigma. As 'escape valves' from tensions at social or personal levels, phenomena like possession states should be left undisturbed by medical attention.

— 4 —

Findings of the Survey—Correlates

DEMOGRAPHY AND ECOLOGY IN MENTAL DISORDERS: GENERAL CONSIDERATIONS

T HE present survey being an epidemiological one, demands that some of the variables, descriptive of the population at risk, be identified first. The importance of these variables from the mental health aspect will be briefly discussed.

Age

From birth defects which result in mental retardation to dementias of old age, correlations between morbidity and age are well established in psychiatric disorders. Schizophrenia type of psychosis usually has its onset in the younger age group, whereas depression is common in older age groups. Mental disorders as a whole tend to increase with advancing age.

Sex

Psychiatric disorders are more common among women, apart from conditions like mental retardation or psychopathy. A high rate of depressive neurosis among women has attracted worldwide attention.

Marital Status

Both age and sex are intricately related to marital status. Differential rates of different disorders are found among single, married, divorced and widowed in western countries. Reliable data in this regard are not available in India.

Social Class

Social class is a widely used concept for ranking or stratifying a total population into subgroups which differ from each other in prestige, wealth, and power . . . . These three dimensions are usually related; a person high in one tends to be high in the others, and vice versa . . . . . The concept of 'class' is a useful summarizing variable linking occupation, education, area of residence, income, and in fact, total life style (Mausner and Bahn, 1974).

Important relationships have been found between social class and mental illness. On the basis of an extensive review of literature, Dohrenwend (1975) concluded that sex, social class and urban-rural differences show a consistent relationship with psychiatric morbidity. However, recent western studies indicate that rural-urban differences are no longer significant (Freeman, 1984). Freeman states that 'it has become a conventional wisdom that low socio-economic status is associated with higher prevalence of psychiatric disorder . . . . but there is no agreement whether this is due to severe stress operating among these classes or due to selection' (that is, genetic and other predisposition or vulnerability to stress).

Occupation and Income

Occupation is often used in epidemiological studies as a measure of the overall socio-economic status. In Britain, five well defined occupations signifying different social classes, are available in Census studies. Income is closely linked with occupation and together they are more or less identical with social class. Certain psychosomatic disorders are associated with different types of occupation.

Urbanisation and Environment

From the early days of psychiatry, a notion had been current that industrialisation and the consequent urbanisation are potent factors in the causation of mental disorders. Industrial societies with their complexities of life style have been compared with simple rural life. Recent studies have focused on the peculiarities of urban living itself, which include poor housing and overcrowding on the one hand and new housing and isolation on the other. Environmental problems such as, noise, vandalism and midtown decay, and social problems like social change, disintegration and alienation, have been studied extensively by sociologists, though there have not been many psychiatric studies in these areas.

The results have been inconclusive, but they have not exonerated these potentially noxious factors. Perhaps we can never find conclusive evidence for the causal association between mental morbidity and environment (Freeman, 1984).

A study in a city like Calcutta, which has been subjected to all the ill effects mentioned earlier on an unprecedented scale and where the processes of urbanisation are still going on unabated, could have offered valuable data on these problems. Unfortunately, we could not cover them in depth; the data on housing, density, etc., collected by the socio-economic team have not been correlated with the mental health data. Other independent variables important in the Indian context, will be discussed later.

PROBLEMS AND METHODS OF COLLECTING DEMOGRAPHIC DATA IN THE SAMPLE POPULATION IN CALCUTTA

Age

It is well known that Indians, particularly the old and the uneducated, are very vague and unconcerned about their age. Indeed, age as recorded by the socio-economic section of the survey teams (aided by the General Physician) was partly guess-work! Since ages of children were fairly well established, we could calculate and verify the ages of their parents.

Sex

Women were more cooperative and were willing to talk about their problems. While men were unwilling to discuss their problems.

Marital Status

There were no problems in ascertaining marital status. In three cases men had two wives. Though the law forbids this, yet the families were unconcerned. We found no evidence of cohabitation (unmarried couples living together) except in one instance. Even if such facts were suppressed, they must have been rare.

Social Class

There is no easy way of determining 'class' in India. The available scales are outdated and somewhat ambiguous. Though education, occupation and income are usually combined to arrive at social class, in India caste adds another dimension. Yet another difficulty in determining class is that at the present stage of rapid social change any computation would place even two members of the same family living together (for example, father and son) into different classes. The father may be illiterate and poor whereas the son may be an educated officer, or the father may be an illiterate, but rich businessman whereas the son may be educated but unemployed. To assign different class status to various members of the same joint family is meaningless, since 'prestige' seems to rest within family units. In our experience, families usually identify with their most educated member. Earlier in

Bengal upper class used to be denoted as *bhadralok* (gentry). *Bhadralok*, needless to say, held mainly non-manual occupations and those involving higher education, like engineering and medicine. In the present study, we have recast occupation as 'occupational status' on the basis of the still current social values of certain occupations. In our classification, high occupational status implied those occupations which only an educated person could hold; a middle status which comprised non-manual as well as manual occupations, such as skilled work. The emerging class of blue collar workers (as they are called in the west) could no longer be thought of as Bengal's traditional non-*bhadralok*, hence this class was considered as middle. According to this classification, low status was assigned to other manual and unskilled workers, as well as to certain caste based occupations.

Occupation

Great care was taken to record the occupation of each member of the family. The Indian Statistical Institute provided a manual which classifies occupations according to a well researched formula based on the nature of the trade or industry as well as groups like manual and non-manual. We deviated from that classification in certain respects. For example, the manager of a shoe factory was listed under 'administrative work' or 'executive' and not under 'leather related work'. Since our aim was to correlate demographic data with different disorders and not their mere enumeration, social values or status of the occupations were considered more important than the nature of the occupations in terms of the work involved. Otherwise housewives would have had either no status or very low status as non-earners, vitiating the value of the important dimension of social class of almost half the sample. Housewives and students were given the status of the family as a whole for cross-tabulation with other variables.

Education

Exact details were noted and initially five groups were identified which were later merged to form three groups. The extent to which people attached importance to education was deduced in an indirect way. To give an opportunity to the families to talk about the positive aspects of their lives, a question was included in the Family Report whether any member had achieved anything outstanding. The answers from the poorer sections often included information about someone who had graduated even if he/she was a very distant relative! Occupation and education together provided the most sensitive indicator of social class.

Economic Strata

The economic and living standards of the families as obtained by computing expenditures were as accurate as possible, as there was no scope for concealing any information. The classification into high, middle and low also reflected the general situation in the population, but the cut-off points involved a blurred area. The expenditure incurred by the whole family per month was divided by the number of family members living in that unit so as to arrive at per capita expenditure. This, however, created a minor problem. A poor family with very few members (e.g., husband and wife) got bracketed with the upper class, whereas a well-to-do family with many members may have been placed with the lower. However, the number of family members was carefully computed with finer economic divisions to arrive at average family size. The discrepancies mentioned above occurred only in the case of a few families (see demographic tables).

Family Type

The type of family, or composition of the family (such as, nuclear and joint) is considered to be very important in the Indian context. Various studies have asserted that joint families facilitate mental health. The difficulty is that there is no simple classification accepted by Indian sociologists, who all seem to have their own classifications. The one adopted by us comes closest to Conklin's (1968) who worked in India and whose classification is very simple (see also Shah, 1973). Nuclear family was defined as husband and wife living with their children, but if one of the parents was dead it was still considered nuclear. Extended family implied that one or two elderly relatives were living as 'dependents' with the nuclear family. It was felt these dependent persons would be looking after the sick members and functioning as 'family support'. Joint family implied that father and sons, or brothers were living together and pooling their resources, and supporting dependent relatives whose role in the joint family could be expected to be less important. Lastly, there are single members either living in their own establishment or living in hostels or institutions. As one can see the main aim of this classification was to determine the support system within the family.

In the initial rounds, the socio-economic team had identified the person whom the family considered as 'head'. We obtained this information from this team and did not question it. However, after the initial analysis, the method adopted for identifying the 'head' and, consequently, for classifying the family types was found to be unsatisfactory and another one was devised. In this second method, the senior most earning member was considered as the 'head' or the 'Index Person' and all others were classified according to their relation to this person, irrespective of whom the family itself designated as the 'head'. It was believed that the 'head' as identified by the family members themselves was being so designated out of sheer politeness in front of strangers. Economic independence or dependence was the key factor in the revised scheme, the details of which will be discussed later.

Family Roles

In keeping with the above mentioned revised scheme, all adults were assigned roles according to their relationship to the 'Index Person' and the exact composition of the family was worked out on that basis.

Location

The survey area covered a radius of 50 miles from the centre of the city. The surrounding area thus included is intimately linked with

Calcutta economically. The suburbs of Calcutta differ in many ways from the city proper. These areas are poorer, with larger concentrations of refugees from the erstwhile East Pakistan. Though nobody carries the refugee status any longer, it remains a sensitive issue with political overtones. For these reasons, investigations were not made into the respondents' possible 'refugee' origins.

There were several small towns located 'outside Calcutta' which had certain distinctive features. The old Bengali residents often own land or property in these areas, mostly old and dilapidated houses, and their cash earnings are minimal. Population densities in these small towns are very high, but these could not be shown separately in our figures, because the land and villages around them reduced the calculation of persons per square mile. Though a considerable number of people commute daily to Calcutta, the character of the suburbs is not like that of European type suburbs or dormitory towns. There are many industries in these areas, jute mills with large concentrations of migrant labour are located on the banks of the Hoogly river. Many mills were closed during the time of the survey due to recession in the industry, leading to unemployment and, consequently, hardship to the local population.

Eight villages from these areas were included in the sample.

Ethnic or Linguistic Groups

Thirty per cent of the population of Calcutta is not local or Bengali-speaking. Though among these non-Bengalis many are migrants from other states, speaking different languages, many of them were born and brought up in Calcutta and are totally assimilated in the local society. This non-Bengali-speaking population was clearly demarcated and was asked questions about their attitudes towards the locals. It is not claimed that they were always cooperative and frank, and discussed their family problems as readily as Bengalis. Family composition of ethnic groups was not determined according to the alternate scheme discussed earlier, as we did not have a good grasp of the intricacies of relationships among them. Also, great variations were seen among them. For instance, Marwari families in Calcutta were very different from the South Indian families.

These different ethnic groups have been considered together for comparison with Bengalis in relation to mental health.

Religion

As with language groups, all major religious communities are also found in Calcutta.

DEMOGRAPHIC CORRELATES OF MENTAL RETARDATION AND EPILEPSY

Summary of Findings in the Sampled Population

Children constituted approximately 32 per cent of the population (N = 4,234).
Male:Female ratio among children was almost equal.
The distribution of children was as follows:

	Low	Middle *(in per cent)*	High
Occupational (Social) Strata	25	44	30
Economic Strata	28	60	12

The distribution of children was slightly higher in nuclear families as compared to joint families, but the child:adult ratio was 1:1 in nuclear and 1:3 in joint families. The distribution of children in Calcutta proper and outside Calcutta was almost the same, though villages had proportionately more children.

Rates of Disorders for Children

Severe Retardation	6/1000
Mild Retardation	19/1000
Epilepsy	6/1000
Conduct Disorder	25/1000
All Disorders Combined	56/1000

1. Severe mental retardation was found to be higher among female children in both 0–5 years and 6–13 years age groups (N.S.) (Tables 4.1 and 4.1a).

TABLE 4.1
Retardation and Epilepsy by Age and Sex
(Percentages are of those of the same sex age groups)

Age Groups (in years)		0–13	14–24	25–39	40–60+	Total	Per cent
Male (Row %)		2163 (29.8)	1641 (22.6)	1660 (22.9)	1771 (24.4)	7235	(100)
Female (Row %)		2071 (33.9)	1408 (23.0)	1326 (22.1)	1295 (21.2)	6100	(100)
Total		4234 (31.7)	3049 (22.8)	2986 (22.3)	3066 (22.9)	13335	(100)
SMR	Male	0.50	0.48	0.24	0.10	25	0.34
	Female	0.72	0.35	0.37	0.07	26	0.42
	Total	0.61	0.42	0.30	0.09	51	0.38
MMR	Male	2.08	2.31	0.24	0.05	88	1.21
	Female	1.73	1.34	0.30	0.15	61	1.00
	Total	1.91	1.86	0.26	0.09	149	1.11
Epilepsy	Male	0.69	1.03	0.30	0.28	42	0.58
	Female	0.57	0.85	0.60	0.38	37	0.60
	Total	0.63	0.95	0.43	0.32	79	0.59
Total	Male	3.28	3.83	0.78	0.45	155	2.14
	Female	3.04	2.55	1.28	0.61	124	2.03
	GT	3.16	3.24	1.00	0.52	279	2.09

TABLE 4.1a
Retardation, Epilepsy and Conduct Disorders in Children
(Percentages are of those of the figures above)

Age Groups	0–5 years		6–13 years	
Sex	Male (783)	Female (760)	Male (1380)	Female (1311)
Severe Mental Retardation	.38	.52	.57	.83
Mild Mental Retardation	.12	.13	3.18	2.60
Epilepsy	.76	.39	.65	.68
Conduct Disorders	.38	.13	6.08	1.30

2. Mild mental retardation was found to be higher among male children in the 6–13 years age group. (N.S.) (Tables 4.1 and 4.1a).

3. Epilepsy was found to be higher among male children in the 0–5 years age group. However, in the 6–13 years age group it was the same for both male and female children (N.S.) (Tables 4.1 and 4.1a).

4. Male – female differences for the three disorders separately or combined were not statistically significant.

5. The number of affected children in the high social status group was less, though not statistically significant.

6. The number of cases of severe retardation was relatively high in the high economic strata (p. <.02) (Table 4.2).

7. The number of cases of mild retardation was high in the middle economic strata (N.S.) (Table 4.2).

8. The number of cases of epilepsy was almost equal in all economic groups (Table 4.2).

9. Both severe retardation and epilepsy were higher in extended families (Table 4.3).

10. The incidence of mild retardation was higher in nuclear families (p. <.01) (Table 4.3).

11. The total number of affected children was less in joint families.

12. Differences in family types for all the affected children were statistically significant (p. <.02) (Table 4.3).

Rates of Disorders for Adults (N = 9,101)

Severe Mental Retardation	2.7/1000
Mild Mental Retardation	7.5/1000
Epilepsy	5.7/1000

TABLE 4.2
Retardation and Epilepsy by Economic Strata
(All Persons)
(Percentages are of those of the figures above)

Economic Strata	Low	Middle	High	Stats Sig.
Children	1194	2516	524	
	(Per cent)	(Per cent)	(Per cent)	
SMR	.83	.35	1.33	<.02
MMR	1.92	2.10	.95	NS
Epilepsy	.67	.63	.57	NS
Total	3.42	3.08	2.85	NS
Adults	1503	5424	2174	
Total	1.33	1.91	.96	<.01
Grand Total	2.26	2.29	1.33	<.01

TABLE 4.3
Mental Retardation and Epilepsy by Family Types
(Percentages are those of the Total Number of Persons in Each Family Type, Unitary
Families Excluded)

Family Type	Nuclear	Extended	Joint	Stats Sig.
Children	(1927)	(585)	(1706)	
Severe Mental Retardation	.51	1.3	.46	N.S.
Mild Mental Retardation	2.50	1.3	1.1	<.01
Epilepsy	.62	.85	.58	N.S.
Total	3.63	3.45	2.14	.02
All Affected				
(Children + Adults)	2.7	2.4	1.6	<.001

1. The majority of cases of severe and mild mental retardation and epilepsy was seen among males in the age group of 14–24 years. (Table 4.1).

2. Two cases of severe retardation were found in the 60+ age group (Table 4.1).

3. Sex differences for these three conditions in adults were not significant.

4. Occupational status differences in the rates of these three conditions did not reach significance.

5. The rates for all the three conditions were highest in the middle economic strata (approximately 60 per cent of the adults comprised the middle strata) (Table 4.2).

6. Economic differences for all the conditions combined were statistically significant (p. < .01) (Table 4.2).
7. A high proportion of disabilities among adults as well as children was seen in extended families (Table 4.3).

Children and Adults (N = 13,335)

1. The proportion of children to adults was almost equal in the case of retardation, but it was 1:2 for epilepsy.
2. The pattern of disorders seen so far was similarly reflected when the total sample was considered.
3. Male—female differences did not show any consistent pattern when the combined disorders were considered for different age groups (Table 4.1).
4. Occupational status differences in the rates of the combined disorders for all persons were statistically significant (p. <.02), the rate being low in high status groups.
5. Economic status differences in the rates of the combined disorders for all persons were statistically significant (p. <.01), the rate being low in high status groups. Mild retardation was also significant (p. <.005) (Table 4.2).
6. Family type differences in the combined disorders for all persons were significant (p. < .001), the rate being low in joint families (Table 4.3).
7. The location or place of residence had little influence on the rates. Both Calcutta proper and areas outside Calcutta had almost similar rates. But epilepsy was unaccountably low in Calcutta slums, whereas it was rather high in villages (Table 4.9).

Discussion

The rate reported for severe retardation among children (4/1000 age adjusted or 6/1000 age specific rate) was close to the lower level of the rate (5–15/1000) found by the research teams of the 'International Pilot Study of Severe Childhood Disability' in developing countries (Belmont, 1984). The rate for mental retardation estimated by the Expert Committee on 'National Mental Health Programme' (1981) was 0.5 to 1 per cent for the child population (or 5 to 10 per 1000);

this probably indicates only the severe types. Another estimate based on various Indian studies, which included mild retardation, was between 13 to 18 million individuals in India, taking the population at 684 million (Prabhu *et al.*, 1985). Our estimate of 1,77,300 retarded persons in a population of 10 million of greater Calcutta would come to a national figure of approximately 13 million as well.

The rate for epilepsy (6/1000) also conforms to that found in developing countries (6–10/1000) by the WHO studies (WHO Technical Report Series, 1978). With the exception of an unaccountably low rate for slums, the rates for epilepsy in our study showed consistency among all sections of the population.

On the whole our estimates of mental retardation and epilepsy are similar to the national and international estimates, a fact which endorses the soundness of our methods which were based on an assessment and judgement of facts (like comparative development and achievements of siblings) and responses of the parents, rather than on tests and measures. The Lucknow study used IQ tests and reported the overall rate for retardation to be 10.2/1000, whereas we observed a rate of 15/1000. The difference, it can be argued, is due to the different levels of cut off point fixed for mild retardation. A test may use an intelligence quotient of 70 as the upper limit of retardation whereas a child may be considered dull even with an IQ of 90, which means non-test assessments may unwittingly adopt a much higher upper limit. The boundaries of mild or borderline retardation are known to be rather blurred; but the utility of expensive tests and procedures in field surveys remains doubtful in the light of near accuracy of non-expensive methods.

The rates observed in Calcutta seem to be at the lower end of the internationally established range of these disorders, which raises the question whether we should have found higher rates in an unhealthy urban area. Retardation is likely to be higher in rural rather than urban areas, because rural birth rate is higher, infection and infestations are more common and medical care is poor. In fact, we did find higher prevalence in the villages, but the sample being small not much importance can be attached to these rates. In industrial areas poisoning (through lead, etc.) and pollution are likely to harm the foetus or the infant, but these effects could not be isolated. However, we agree that the low rate for severe retardation is rather suspect although such low rates have been found in many other studies in India (Prabhu *et al.*, 1985). Maternal factors that are harmful to the foetus in utero (poor nutrition, infection, ill health, etc.) are undoubtedly high in a poor country like India and should have produced retardation on a higher scale across the nation but, on the contrary, consistent low rates have been reported. The reasons may be protection by an as yet unidentified genetic factor, the possibility of the defective foetus being easily aborted due to poor ante-natal care, lower prevalence of genetically determined conditions, high early mortality, infanticide or benign neglect of the retarded child to hasten death. The latter is more likely to be seen in the case of female children in India as male children are highly valued. As yet, we have no unequivocal indication towards any of these possibilities.

Mild retardation as a subject often evokes controversy, the concept is thought to be relative depending on the social demands and expectations. It is possible that in an undemanding agricultural society, many deficiencies would go unnoticed, which could perhaps be the reason for the low rate of retardation in India. In western countries on the other hand a rate as high as 200/1000 has been recorded (Stein and Susser, 1975). However, we feel that in India, the various masking effects do not depress the rate, but it is genuinely so.

The higher rate for SMR among female children is at variance with other Indian studies (Prabhu *et al.*, 1985). As this rate is higher even in the 0–5 years age group, it suggests the possibility that defective male children have higher early mortality, or conversely, that female infanticide (through neglect) is higher in other parts of India. However, as stillbirths and early deaths were not investigated, we cannot comment on any disorder in children below 5 years of age. Hence, the high female rates for both the age groups remain unexplained. Mild retardation is seldom detected or admitted by parents before the child enters school, which accounts for the very low rate at the lower age levels. Boys between 6–13 years of age outnumber girls in both mild retardation and conduct disorder. This disparity is a universal finding and is probably caused by both biological and social factors.

The higher rate for SMR in the upper economic strata was surprising but understandable. These cases probably had better chances of survival in affluent homes. All the three conditions combined had lower rates in the high economic strata as well as in the high occupational (which has been taken as social status) group. This may be accounted for by the better treatment available for epileptics and better educational assistance for the mildly retarded in these classes. As stated earlier, the label of mild retardation may be nothing more than the demands and expectations of the environment on the child. Aspiring middle class parents usually attach high value to educational competence and may be inclined to consider their children 'dull' when they fail to meet their expectations. Higher rates for MMR were observed in the middle economic strata, but this 'diagnosis' was not solely based on the labelling given by parents. To assess the level of aspiration and educational incompetence in the community, questions were asked regarding school performance and it was found that 5 per cent of the literate population 'did not do well in school'. School records posed further problems; most children were attending school, as schools were free up to Class VI or 10 years of age. (Today, schools offer free education up to Class X.) Some retarded children continued to attend school up to the age of ten, which made them appear more educable than they actually were. This implied that the moderately retarded in this study were placed in the mild category. Careful attention was paid to ascertain the various aspects of retardation. As in the case of mild retardation and conduct disorders, educational backwardness was also observed to be more common among middle class male children.

The higher rates for all conditions in nuclear families as compared to joint families may have been a reflection of the higher number or proportion of children in nuclear families. It is also possible that the rates are low in joint families because pregnant wives or young mothers receive better attention, care and advice, but this seems rather doubtful. It has been observed (WHO/SEA 1978) that having elderly female relatives in the family helps in the survival of the disabled, because they assist in looking after the disabled. Though the rates of retardation were found to be higher in families where such persons were present (transitional or extended families) as compared to families where they were not (nuclear families), we feel that the observation of WHO/SEA (1978) is extremely unlikely to be the reason; we found a high level of morbidity among dependent relatives. Sick people are not likely to be able to look after other sick persons (see the discussion on family roles, etc.).

Some cases of mild retardation were also found in institutions (unitary households). A retarded boy was working in a tea shop and the owner looked after him.

The quality of the environment differs between Calcutta and the outlying areas. The atmospheric pollution is less, but in other respects the outlying areas are more unhealthy, towns are densely populated, water and sanitation facilities are poorer, general health standard is lower and the level of poverty is higher. However, there was not much difference in retardation rates. As stated earlier, rural rates were higher and slum rates were lower than the average. A study (Sen *et al.*, 1984) in a Calcutta slum (population 2,000) reported the rate for mental retardation to be 5/1000 and for epilepsy 3.4/1000; our rates for slums were 10/1000 and 2.4/1000 respectively. These low rates for epilepsy in slums are rather surprising and remain unexplained, but the high rate in the villages is probably related to parasitic infestations.

Children in the lower economic strata had poor health, severe deficiency as well as other diseases. But not a single case was detected where vitamin deficiency or other diseases were directly contributory to mental retardation or epilepsy (see Health of the Population).

The detection of retardation cases was facilitated by the parents' efforts to seek help. They consulted doctors and healers as well as the survey teams. It may also be mentioned here that all children in the sample were physically examined and interviewed, informants, usually parents, only supplied the details. Hence, no case went unnoticed because of lack of awareness on the part of 'key' informants, which is often what happens in this type of survey.

DEMOGRAPHIC CORRELATES OF PSYCHOSES AND RELATED DISORDERS

Summary of Findings in the Sampled Population

Some important demographic features of the adult sampled persons (N = 9101).

1. Age distribution among females showed that a higher proportion was at the lower age levels, and there was a considerable reduction in the number of females at the 40–59 years age level.
2. Sex ratio—male:female—showed much variation in all age groups; it varied from 1.1 to 1.6. In the 'over 60 years' age group the ratio was almost equal. The overall percentages were 54.7 and 44.3 for males and females respectively. Among Bengalis

these were 53.1 per cent and 46.8 per cent, among non-Bengalis 62.4 per cent and 37.5 per cent.

3. There were few younger and more older people in the higher economic group, the reverse was true for the lower economic strata.

4. There were more females who were poor than males, particularly those living outside Calcutta.

5. Areas outside Calcutta proper had a higher proportion of poor people than Calcutta 'proper'.

6. There were proportionately more females than males at the low educational level.

7. There were more non-Bengalis than Bengalis at the low educational level, the difference being most marked among females.

Summary of Findings

The rate for active psychosis was 7/1000 of the adult sample population.

The rate for abnormal personality and paranoid states was 12/1000 of the adult sample population.

Psychoses rates seem to rise steadily with advancing age, but fall off at the age of 60 years and above. The association of age with disorder was significant (Table 4.4).

The rates were higher for females at all age levels, with the exception of 14–24 years age group (Table 4.4).

The peak periods for psychoses, etc., were 50–59 years for males and 40–49 years for females (Table 4.4).

The 'increase with age' pattern was found among both males and females for most types of psychoses and related disorders. However, in the case of males with active psychosis, the rate showed an increasing trend instead of a decrease at the age of 60 years and above (Table 4.5).

The typical 'age effect' was observed among both males and females with different marital status.

The same age effect was also seen in relation to different economic and educational strata; however, the trend was more consistent at the upper levels of both the variables than for males at the lower levels.

Sex difference was highly significant in active psychosis, it was more in the case of female psychotics. However, it was not significant in 'related disorders', the rate being almost similar (Table 4.6).

TABLE 4.4
Psychoses, etc., and Psychoneuroses by Age and Sex
(Percentages of disorders are those of the same sex age groups)

Age Groups (in years)	14–24	Per cent	25–39	Per cent	40–49	Per cent	50–59	Per cent	60 +	Per cent	Total	Per cent
Male Row %	1641	32.3	1660	32.7	816	16.0	561	11.0	394	7.7	5072	(100)
Female Row %	1408	34.9	1326	32.9	555	13.7	348	8.6	392	9.7	4029	(100)
Total Row (%)	3049	33.5	2986	32.8	1371	15.0	909	9.9	786	8.9	9101	(100)
Psychoses and Related Disorder												
Male	23	1.40	20	1.20	18	2.20	16	2.85	10	2.53	87	1.71[1]
Female	13	.92	34	2.56	21	3.78	12	3.44	11	2.80	91	2.25[2]
Total	36	1.18	54	1.80	39	2.84	28	3.08	21	2.69	178	1.95
Psychoneuroses												
Male	81	4.93	98	5.90	61	7.47	53	9.44	53	13.45	346	6.82[3]
Female	124	8.80	226	17.04	120	21.62	78	22.4	104	26.53	652	16.18[4]
Total	205	6.72	324	10.85	181	13.20	131	14.4	157	19.97	998	10.95

[1] Chi Sq. 9.4 df 4 p. <.05   [3] Chi Sq. 45.2 df 4 p. <.001
[2] Chi Sq. 19.4 df 4 p. <.001   [4] Chi Sq. 110.2 df 4 p. <.001

TABLE 4.5
Different Psychoses and Related Disorders by Age and Sex
(Percentages are those of the same sex age groups)

Age Groups (in years)		(14–24)	(25–39)	(40–49)	(50–59)	(60+)	Total
Paranoid State	Male	.12	.30	.49	.35	.25	.27
	Female	.21	.70	.90	.57	.76	.57
Abnormal Personality	Male	1.03	.66	.85	1.78	.76	.94
	Female	.21	.60	1.44	.86	.76	.62
'Disturbed' Psychosis	Male	.06	.06	.24	0	.50	.11
	Female	.21	.37	.54	1.14	.51	.42
'Quiet' Psychosis	Male	.12	.18	.36	.35	.50	.23
	Female	.14	.75	.72	.57	.25	.47
'Depressed' Psychosis	Male	.06	0	.24	.35	.50	.13
	Female	.14	.07	.18	.28	.51	.17
Psychoses and Related Disorders	Male	1.40	1.20	2.20	2.85	2.53	1.71
	Female	.92	2.56	3.78	3.44	2.80	2.25
Total		1.18	1.80	2.84	3.08	2.69	1.95

TABLE 4.6
Significance of Sex Differences in Psychoses and Related Disorders and Psychoneuroses and Related Disorders
(Percentages are of those of the figures above)

	Male	Female	Chi Sq.	df.	P.
	(5072)	(4029)			
Psychoses	25 (.49)	43 (1.06)	9.99	1	<.005
Related Disorders	62 (1.22)	48 (1.19)			N.S.
Total	87 (1.71)	91 (2.25)	3.46	1	N.S.
Psychoneuroses	346 (6.82)	652 (16.18)	201.52	1	<.001
Related Disorders	37 (.72)	167 (4.14)	119.53	1	<.001
Total	470 (9.26)	910 (22.5)	319.74	1	<.001

Males showed higher rates for abnormal personality in most age groups and for 'depressed' psychosis in the 40–60 years age group.

Unmarried males showed higher rates in all age groups, except in the 14–24 years age group, where married men had a higher rate, and this was even higher than that observed among married females of the same age group.

Both unmarried and married females did not show any consistent pattern of psychoses in relation to age.

Higher rates were observed among unmarried and married males as compared to females but lower rates were observed among widowers (Table 4.7a).

TABLE 4.7a
Psychoses, etc., and Psychoneuroses by Marital Status and Sex
(Percentages are of those of the figures above)

Marital Status	Single	Married	Widow/Widower
Male	2025	2957	90
Psychoses	1.7	1.6	2.2
Neuroses	5.5	7.5	11.1
Female	1017	2462	550
Psychoses	1.2	1.1	3.6
Neuroses	7.8	16.6	29.2

Comparison between different economic strata revealed the highest overall rate for males in the low economic strata and for females in the middle strata. However, the economic differences were not statistically significant (Table 4.8).

TABLE 4.7b

Combined Psychoses, etc., and Psychoneuroses by Marital Status and Sex: Ratio of Observed to Expected Number of Affected Persons

Marital Status	Males		Females	
	Number of Patients	Ratio Per cent	Number of Patients	Ratio Per cent
Single	148	108.0	93	81.1
Married	273	96.3	469	97.9
Widow/Widower	12	99.9	181	122.0
Total	433	100.0	743	100.0

Note: Age was standardised. The expected numbers were calculated on the assumption that, within each age group, there was no association between marital status and mental disorders.

TABLE 4.8

Psychoses, Related Disorders and Psychoneuroses by Economic Strata and Sex
(Percentages are of those of the figures above)

Economic Strata	Low		Middle		High	
	Male (772)	Female (731)	Male (3048)	Female (2376)	Male (1252)	Female (922)
Paranoid State	.38	.41	.32	.50	.07	.86
Abnormal Personality	1.4	.54	.95	.63	.63	.65
Psychoses	.38	.68	.41	1.38	.69	.53
	2.2	1.64	1.7	2.5	1.40	2.04
Psychoneuroses	6.6	17.5	7.3	16.4	5.5	14.3
(Combined Male + Female)						
	Male + Female (1503)		Male + Female (5424)		Male + Female (2174)	
Psychoses and Related Disorders	1.9		2.0		1.7 [1]	
Psychoneuroses	11.9		11.3		9.2 [2]	
Total	13.8		13.4		10.9 [3]	

Stats. Sig. [1] N.S.   [2] Chi Sq. 8.52   df 2 p. <.02
               [3] Chi Sq. 6.55   df 2 p. <.05

Higher rates for 'abnormal personality' were observed among males from low and middle economic strata; females from high strata had the highest rate for paranoid state. The highest rates for active psychosis were observed in the high and middle strata for males and females respectively (Table 4.8).

(None of the above conditions among males or females or together were significantly associated with economic strata).

Areas outside Calcutta reported a higher rate for psychoses (N.S.); the rate in the villages was higher than that observed in Calcutta slums (Table 4.9).

Combined psychoses and psychoneuroses rates revealed that all economic strata outside Calcutta had higher rates. Stratum-wise comparison of location showed highly significant associations for the lower and middle strata but not for the upper strata (Table 4.10).

Higher rates for abnormal personality and active psychosis and only marginally lower rate for paranoid condition were observed in the case of low occupational status. However, the associations were not significant (Table 4.11).

Higher rates for different categories of psychoses and related disorders were observed among both males and females with low education, with the exception of the category of 'depressed psychosis' where males with high education had a slightly higher rate than other males (Table 4.12a).

Educational differences in psychoses were highly significant for both males (p. < .01) and females (p. < .001), the poorly educated people were more affected (Table 4.12b).

A much higher rate for psychoses was observed among Bengalis as compared to non-Bengalis. The difference was more marked among females (Table 4.13).

Non-Bengalis in all educational categories showed a much lower rate; non-Bengali females in the low education group showed a higher rate.

Extended families had the highest overall rate for psychoses and related disorders followed by nuclear families. Joint families had the lowest overall rate; the differences in these rates were not statistically significant (Table 4.14a & 4.14b).

DISCUSSION ON THE CORRELATES OF PSYCHOSES FOUND BY THE SURVEY

Age

In keeping with the findings of large scale surveys, the present one showed an increase in the rates of psychoses with age and subsequent

TABLE 4.9
Mental Disorders by Location
(Percentages are of those of the figures above)

All Persons	Calcutta	Slums	Total	Outside Calcutta	Villages	Total	Sig.
	(6567)	(831)	(7398)	(5010)	(927)	(5937)	P.
Mental Retardation	1.59	1.08		1.3	1.8		
Epilepsy	.67	.24		.51	.75		
Total			160 (2.1)			119 (2.0)	N.S.
Adults	4705	550		3291	555		
Psychoses, etc.	1.97	1.45		2.0	1.98		N.S.
Psychoneuroses	9.54	10.72		12.91	11.71		<.001
Total			609 (11.58)			567 (14.7)	<.001

TABLE 4.10
Combined Psychoses, etc., and Psychoneuroses by Location and Economic Strata
(Percentages are of those of the figures above)

Economic Strata	Low	Middle	High	
Calcutta	700	2958	1957	5255
Affected	75	365	169	N.S.[1]
	(10.7)	(12.1)	(10.5)	(11.5)
Outside Calcutta	803	2466	577	3486
Affected	133	364	70	N.S.[2]
	(16.5)	(14.7)	(12.1)	(14.7)
	X^2 10.72	X^2 6.77	X^2 1.03	
	p. <.001[3]	p. <.01[4]	N.S.[5]	

Note:

[1] and [2] Chi Sq. tests between different economic strata of affected and non-affected adults—not significant.

[3] and [4] Chi Sq. tests between different locations but within the same strata of affected and not affected adults—highly significant.

[5] Chi Sq. test within high strata—not significant.

TABLE 4.11
Different Mental Disorders by Occupational Status
(Percentages are of those of the figures above)

Occupational Status	Low	Middle	High	Sig.
Adults	1853	3505	3743	p.
Possession State	.70	.56	.24	<.05
Suchi-bai	.91	1.96	2.03	<.01
Paranoid State	.43	.48	.32	
Abnormal Personality	1.02	.71	.77	
Psychoses	.91	.88	.53	
	2.36	2.07	1.62	N.S.
Neuroses	12.91	11.81	9.58	<.005

fall at 60 years and over. The same trend was also observed with regard to schizophrenia and manic-depressive psychosis by Dube (1970). Shepherd *et al.* (1981) have explained this trend as an accumulation effect, as only chronic type of cases are usually detected in point prevalence type of population surveys. 'Chronic cases found in younger age groups are maintained throughout the middle years; in the over sixties, the fall in new cases more than balance the accumulation of chronic cases' Shepherd *et al.* (1981).

The trend is a strong one and becomes apparent in every kind of

TABLE 4.12a

Different Disorders by Sex and Educational Levels

(Percentages are of those of the figures above)

Educational Groups	Low		Middle		High	
Adults	Male (1161)	Female (1605)	Male (2138)	Female (1710)	Male (1773)	Female (714)
Possession State	.51	1.1	.18	.64	.05	.28
Suchi-bai	.60	3.8	.46	3.5	.50	1.9
Paranoid State	.51	.68	.32	.46	.05	.56
Abnormal Personality	1.6	1.0	.88	.55	.56	.28
Disturbed Psychosis	.25	.87	.04	.17	.11	—
Quiet Psychosis	.34 } .67	.80 } 1.9	.14 } .22	.17 } .51	.28 } .67	.42 } .42
Depressed Psychosis	.08	.24	.04	.17	.28	—
Neuroses	7.9	20.6	6.7	15.0	6.1	8.8
Total	11.8	29.2	8.8	20.6	8.0	12.3

TABLE 4.12b
Psychoses, etc., and Psychoneuroses by Educational Levels and Sex
(Statistical Significance)

Educational Groups	Low	Middle	High	p.
Males				
Psychoses	2.84	1.44	1.29	<.01
Neuroses	7.92	6.78	6.14	N.S.
Females				
Psychoses	3.67	1.3	1.26	<.001
Neuroses	20.6	15.08	8.82	<.001

TABLE 4.13
Psychoses, etc., and Psychoneuroses by Ethnic Groups and Sex
(Percentages are of those of the figures above)

Bengalis	Males (3473)	Females (3066)	Total (6539)
Psychoses	1.9	2.4	2.1
Neuroses	8.2	17.4	12.5
Non-Bengalis	(1599)	(963)	(2562)
Psychoses	1.2	1.6	1.4
Neuroses	3.7	12.0	6.8

group, provided the number of cases is large. In the present study the trend was quite clearly seen in the overall rates as well as in many other rates, with the exception of the rate of active psychosis among males. There are several possible reasons for the latter. First, the smallness of the number of male psychotics, which resulted from the previously discussed method of categorisation; when 'psychosis related disorders' (or abnormal personality and paranoid state, which were found in sizeable numbers among males) were added to the rate of active psychosis, the 'age effect' was clear. Second, more new cases than expected were added to the age group of 60 years and above. Such cases could have been depressions of old age; we did observe more male depression cases in a higher age group, particularly among the educated. However, the indication of increased vulnerability of older men to late onset psychoses is only tentative as the number of cases was low.

In a later section we have argued in favour of better prognosis

TABLE 4.14a
Different Disorders by Family Types
(Percentages are of those of the figures above)

Family Types	Nuclear	Extended	Joint	Single	Total
Row (%)	2499 (27.4%)	1221 (13.4%)	5034 (55.3%)	347 (3.8%)	9101 (100%)
Possession State	.28	.90	.43	.57	.46
Suchi-bai	1.8	2.0	1.6	1.7	1.78
Paranoid State	.56 ⎫	.49 ⎫	.31 ⎫	.28 ⎫	.40 ⎫
Abnormal Personality	.72 ⎬ 2.0	1.2 ⎬ 2.5	.75 ⎬ 1.8	.57 ⎬ 1.13	.80 ⎬ 1.94
Psychoses	.72 ⎭	.81 ⎭	.75 ⎭	.28 ⎭	.74 ⎭
Neuroses	11.8	14.9	9.5	10.6	10.9
Total	15.9	20.4	13.3	14.1	15.1

TABLE 4.14b
Psychoses and Psychoneuroses, etc., by Family Types
(Unitary Families are Excluded)
(Statistical Significance)

Family Types	Nuclear	Extended	Joint	Total	p.
Adults	2499	1221	5034	8754	
Psychoses	50	31	93		N.S.
Psychoneuroses	349	219	589		<.0001

(outcome) of psychoses in Indians; good prognosis may account for the low prevalence of psychoses, that is, less accumulation, but it does not explain the anomalous 'age effect' in males.

Sex and Marital Status

Women were found to outnumber men in all conditions apart from 'abnormal personality'. That a high rate for this condition was found among young males, raises the possibility of it being similar to schizophrenia (which is common among young males in other cultures). We have discussed the possibility of 'abnormal personality' being an arrested form of psychosis; perhaps cases would be diagnosed as schizophrenia elsewhere or these cases could develop into schizophrenias, depending on the socio-cultural environment. The combined rate for 'abnormal personality' and active psychoses was found to be higher among young males as compared to that among young females, which made the trend in psychoses in Calcutta consistent with the findings elsewhere.

The rates for married men and women were high in the younger age group (14–24 years). This finding requires some explanation because it is not a usual observation.

In India it is difficult to comment on the influence of marriage as it is usually 'arranged'. Relatives and well-wishers frequently recommend marriage of young persons suffering from mental illness for its supposed 'therapeutic value'. (They may not have been wrong after all as marriage does seem to provide some protective function for men, though it is more stressful for women.) For the high rates noted here, it has been postulated that such social intervention had 'forced' young psychotics of both sexes to get married; marriage could also have acted as a precipitant of psychoses in young females.

In other age groups, and in agreement with the findings elsewhere, the unmarried showed higher rates than the married. This was possibly due to the lack of opportunities to get married because of the illness or because of unemployment.

Divorced or separated persons were clubbed together with widows or widowers as the number of such people was very small. It was also observed that the number of widowers were very few as compared to widows (the proportion was 1:5), the reason being the wide disparity in age that usually exists in arranged marriages, the husbands being much older die earlier. Widowhood was found to be very stressful with loss of spouse at an early age being even more so (for further discussion see the section on psychoneurosis).

Income, Education, Occupation

It goes without saying that these three variables are closely related. Poor people with little education also have low occupational status. However, a consistent pattern of psychoses in relation to these variables was not observed in this study.

Active psychosis was found to be more common among females in middle to lower economic strata, while males in the upper strata were more affected. But these rates were counterbalanced by the high rate of paranoid state among females in the upper strata and 'abnormal personality' among males in the lower strata. Since these diagnostic categories were rather loose, there is no justification in treating them separately in relation to the variables,also, the number of such categorised cases if divided into ecological sub-groups were too few (often nil) in each set to draw meaningful conclusions. Hence, only the overall rate of active psychosis together with the related disorders is being taken into account for purposes of discussion.

It was seen that males from low economic, educational and occupational levels had higher rates, but apart from the association with education no other was statistically significant. In females educational differences were highly significant but not the other differences. The rates for females were higher in the middle strata of both income and occupation groups.

The possibility that non-Bengalis (or migrants and other groups who constituted a large proportion of the poorly educated) had an influence on the significant result regarding the educational variable, was eliminated by considering them separately. It was found that high rates of psychoses in the low education levels were present in both Bengalis (markedly so) and in non-Bengalis. So, no extraneous stress factor such as migration was involved.

Areas outside Calcutta faced more acute economic problems as compared to Calcutta. Hence these areas were computed and tested separately. Again, though the rate was high in the low economic strata, the differences between strata were not significant. However, it was found that these areas were more distressed (see discussion on psychoneuroses).

Gross psychoses were more common among women, but taking the variant forms into account, the overall rates were not significantly different from those for males. Women belonging to the middle and upper socio-economic strata were observed to be more vulnerable, but this finding was anomalous because these affected women had a low level of education. It is difficult to explain this finding. Though there was a high correlation between education and income, it goes without saying that there were some women (particularly elderly widows) in affluent families who were poorly educated. It would be rather far-fetched to suggest that these women were mainly affected, but the high rate of paranoid state in the high strata is a suggestive finding. Paranoid ideas have been found to be widely prevalent in Bengali culture (Chakraborty and Bhattacharya, 1985). Paranoia may act as a defence against insecurity and 'powerlessness' where these are felt more acutely, which was possibly true in the case of economically dependent, poorly educated women of the upper class.

Considering these three variables together there seems to be a fairly clear indication that psychoses are more common among males in the lower strata of the population, but the trend is just the opposite among females with the upper levels being more affected.

These results are anomalous and confusing. If we believe that socio-economic factors play a part in the causation of mental disorders then we have to seek further explanation for their differential effect on the sexes. At the local level, we feel that these results could have been influenced by the disparity in sex ratio that is seen in the Calcutta population, particularly in the 40–59 years age group. There are few women of the lower strata in this age group. There could of course be many other reasons.

As mentioned earlier, Bengal is witnessing profound social change, involving class, caste, sex roles, etc. It is likely that different groups are facing different kinds of stressors. It has been suggested that there is both a sex difference as well as a class difference in the way psycho-social stresses are handled (Murphy, 1983; Kessler, 1979). Perhaps women from more affluent homes could 'afford' to become psychotic while the poorer ones manifested their anxiety-depressive symptoms in a neurotic fashion. In addition, Kessler's (1979) suggestions about class difference in experiencing stress, whereby upper classes withstand more but ultimately 'break rather than bend', and that education (besides other factors like social support) facilitates the use and learning of coping strategies, may be of relevance here. In the present study, class and sex differences in naming and labelling could have played a significant part as well.

As Freeman (1984) has observed, it may never be possible to relate mental disorders to socio-economic conditions. Hence, it would have been important if a clear indication could be found linking psychoses with economic strata in this city with its appalling poverty. However, as far as psychoses are concerned, we found only tentative and partial indications towards that association.

DEMOGRAPHIC CORRELATES OF PSYCHONEUROSES AND RELATED DISORDERS

Summary of Findings in the Sampled Population

The Individual Report Schedule (IRS) was used as a neuroses screening questionnaire (for validity studies, see Appendix III), conditions not detected by it—possession states and *suchi-bai*—are considered as 'related disorders'.

Nearly 150 reports were considered unreliable (including those from severely disordered persons), and some 225 persons could not be contacted or refused to answer questions. They were not excluded from the total of sampled adults for convenience of computation.

Summary of Findings

The rates for both males and females increased with advancing age. The age differences were highly significant (Table 4.4). The ratio of affected females to males was almost 2:1.

Male/female differences in rates were highly significant (Table 4.6). The increase in the rates of psychoneuroses with age, reached the peak, for both males and females, at the age of 60 years and over, unlike that in psychoses which showed a fall at this age. This pattern was consistent in all economic strata, somewhat varied in the educational groups and totally inconsistent in different marital status groups (Table 4.4).

The rates for widows and widowers were higher than those for married persons. The unmarried had the lowest rate in the overall figures (Table 4.7a).

The male:female differences in marital status in age adjusted combined rates indicated that widows had a higher observed to expected ratio (M:F—99.9:122); unmarried males also had a high ratio (M:F—108:81); while it was almost equal in the case of married men and women. (100 was taken as the index figure expected on the overall average) (Table 4.7b).

In terms of economic differences, the rates were higher for males in the middle strata and for females in the lower strata. However, the differences were not significant for either; but when the rates for males and females were combined, the association was significant (p. < .02), and there was lower incidence of neuroses in the upper strata (Table 4.8).

Male and female rates separately were, however, strongly associated with the economic strata in certain age groups. There was a significant association between neuroses and the age group of 40–49 years in the case of males (p. < .05), as well as females (p. < .01). The rates were high in the middle strata and low strata for males and females respectively. The rates were low in the upper strata for both males and females. Similar rates and significance levels were also noted in the case of females between 25–39 years of age.

Location and neuroses were significantly associated in the overall figures (p. < .001) (Table 4.9).

The combined rates for psychoses and neuroses outside Calcutta were much higher in all the economic groups. In Calcutta the rate reported in the case of the middle strata was slightly higher, but outside Calcutta the rate observed in the lower strata was much higher than that seen in the other groups (Table 4.10). The association of neuroses with economic strata was not significant in either location. However, when each stratum was considered separately for areas within Calcutta and those outside Calcutta, highly significant associations were found. Persons in the middle and lower strata living outside Calcutta were more affected. The probabilities were < .01 and < .001 respectively. However, in the upper strata the association was not significant (Table 4.10).

Low and high occupational status groups showed higher rates of possession state and *suchi-bai* respectively. Psychoneuroses were high in the low status group; and this finding was highly significant (p. < .005) (Table 4.11). Rates for males and females in the low educational group were high. The educational differences were significant in the case of females but not in the case of males. (Table 4.12a and 4.12b).

Rates for possession states and *suchi-bai* were higher in the low educational group (Table 4.12a).

The increase in the rates of psychoneuroses with age were highly significant in the low and middle educational groups (p. < .001), but not in the high strata.

Non-Bengali men and women had much lower rates for psychoneuroses than Bengalis of either sex. This was also true in the case of all educational groups (Table 4.13).

Extended type of families showed higher rates of psychoneuroses, as well as possession states and *suchi-bai*. Nuclear families had higher rates as compared to joint families, and this finding was highly significant (Tables 4.14a and 4.14b).

Females holding low level occupations had higher rates of neuroses, followed by non-earners, low-middle, housewives and high-middle occupations (Table 5.14).

Non-earning males had higher rate of neuroses than other males (Table 5.14).

Discussion

(See also discussion under psychotic disorders.) We have discussed at length the difficulties in labelling respondents in a field survey as clinical cases. Though only the severe type of complaints with other associated features were labelled neuroses, it must be reiterated that these indicated only potential cases. However, whatever may have been the nomenclature, this group of individuals did distinguish themselves in having common characteristics which were in keeping with such groups elsewhere, lending a considerable measure of validity to this study, in spite of the fact that its concept and methodology were so different.

As stated earlier, the most consistent finding in psychiatric investigations has been the vulnerability of women to psychiatric disorders. Almost all studies have reported a high prevalence of minor psychiatric disorders among women, where the male:female ratio has been 1 : 2, which was observed in the present study as well. Another finding that is supported by other studies was the increase in minor psychiatric disorders with age. In psychoses, chronicity perhaps accounted for this increase. However, in neuroses, longstanding cases were separately categorised as neurotic personality; hence, accumulation could not be the reason. Economic insecurity in old age was not the reason either, because economic condition did not alter this trend. Hence, in all probability, advancing age enhanced inherent vulnerability.

Widowhood made the wor ...n more predisposed to neuroses. Since widows are found in large numbers at a later age when neuroses are also common, a calculation was designed (following Shepherd *et al.*, 1981) to eliminate the age factor and to obtain a true picture. It was found that there were more widows than expected (see Table 4.7b) suffering from mental disorders (rates for psychoses and psychoneuroses were combined for purposes of calculation). The high rate among widows could have been due to the loss of status and feeling of insecurity that are concomitants of widowhood, but such reasoning does not explain why young widowers (though only a few were found) were so distressed. Perhaps, marriage is still held as sacrosanct and a matter of fate in our country.

The calculation mentioned earlier showed that unmarried males were more affected, a finding which was not unexpected (see the discussion on psychoses), but the low vulnerability observed among single females requires some explanation. Spinsterhood is supposed to carry a social stigma, which may be perceived as a stressor by women, but apparently it did not influence the rates. However, in the present sample, there were very few unmarried women in the older age groups, a fact which could have influenced the results. Hence, it is difficult to comment on this finding. All the same, changing social and sex roles and growing economic independence of many educated women may have belied some old assumptions. This problem will be discussed later.

The finding that men and women of the lower income strata in the 40–49 years age group were more affected could have been related to migration and subsequent change in family life. A considerable reduction (probably comparative) in the female population was found in the over 40s group which could have been caused by the influx of male migrant workers from different states and local villages in search of jobs (a feature seen in all large cities), leaving their women folk behind. (Perhaps such women in the 25–39 years age group in the hinterland of Calcutta were affected in excess.)

The large discrepancy in rates between people living in Calcutta and those living in the suburbs seems to be related to higher levels of poverty prevailing outside Calcutta. As stated earlier, there were more poor and less affluent people outside Calcutta. But the situation was complex. The overall rate outside Calcutta was higher and significant, but the association of the disorders was not with poverty as such, or in other words, with the poor compared to the rich. It was only when one set of poor was compared with another set that the difference became significant, but this was not so when the two sets of the upper strata were compared. Hence, we can postulate that living in the suburbs of Calcutta is more stressful and that these stresses affect the poor and middle classes more than the upper class.

One simple reason needs to be excluded before emphasising the above statement, that is, the finding under discussion could have been influenced by the discrepancies in male-female distribution in different strata and locations. There were indeed larger number of women in the lower strata than in the upper strata outside Calcutta and more women than men were affected in these areas (as elsewhere). However, where such discrepancy did not occur, as in the middle strata, the rate outside Calcutta was significantly higher as well.

It was difficult to isolate the stress factors outside Calcutta. Of the various possibilities that were examined, one was migration. We found that non-Bengalis, both males and females, in different economic and educational strata, as well as in different locations, had much lower rates. Thus, the usual type of migration was not the cause. There was another type of migrants, or 'refugees' in these areas, those who came from erstwhile East Pakistan at the time of Independence. These people no longer carried a refugee status, and for reasons explained earlier, not much information was elicited about the origin of the people living around Calcutta. Assimilation had been difficult for these people (Chakraborty, 1978) and possibly they were still vulnerable. The suggestion is a tentative one, but Sethi *et al.* (1972) have also considered the problems of 1947 refugees as having their own peculiar characteristics. It may be mentioned that the people under discussion were 'refugees' of 1947 and not the temporary ones who came consequent to the creation of Bangladesh in 1971.

The association of neuroses with economic conditions was found to be variable; the evidence here was stronger than in the case of psychoses that poorer women suffered more, but the indications were not absolutely clear. There was also a definite association with occupational and educational strata, specially in the case of females, neuroses being higher in the low strata.

The relation between certain occupations and neuroses in women perhaps reflects the high rates in the low status-low education group of women. Low rates among female students compared to housewives in general again emphasises the low level of risk among single and younger women.

Small, nuclear and extended families had higher neuroses rates than joint and large families. The finding supports the much lauded joint family system in India. However, here we found an unusual feature: high prevalence of all disorders in extended or transitional families (these are 'in-between' nuclear and joint families). (Detailed discussion regarding this is to be found in the sections on family and occupation which elaborate on the effect of work and family roles in the genesis of complaints.)

Possession state was more common in women of low status and with poor education. These findings agree with our clinical impression that possession state was almost never seen in the upper levels of society, whereas *suchi-bai* was probably more common among high caste older women, which explains the high status-low education background found in the present study.

It would appear that women belonging to the lower strata of society were more vulnerable to social stresses, resulting in more neurotic complaints. In the case of men, not only were the complaints far less, but no associations were found with demographic factors.

We may conclude that women were observed to be most vulnerable, particularly those belonging to the lower strata of society and those in the older age groups. Education affords some protection against stress as do joint families (though there could be other explanations). People living outside Calcutta, particularly the lower and middle income groups, were more vulnerable. Bengalis suffered more than migrants and other groups.

Though this study accorded support to the present almost universal finding that women of low socio-economic status are vulnerable to minor psychiatric disorders, it was not able to ascertain any particular causal factor. Besides biological vulnerability (Murphy, 1983), an excess of traumatic life events have been said to be a potent factor underlying depression in these women (Brown and Harris, 1978). It is to be noted that the sub-type of neuroses most common in our 'cases' was anxiety-depressive type of complaints. We generally agree to this view, and a later chapter by Sandel is devoted to the study of life-events and difficulties among women of Calcutta (though on a small sample). However, we feel that coping strategies, which are based on cultural learning, may be inadequate due to different reasons. Pluri-causality, that is, similar results through different causes have been suggested by Murphy (1982).

5

Mental Health of the Families and Special Groups

FAMILIES, ROLES AND NEUROSES

JOINT families are hallowed institutions in India. Indian psychiatrists attach great importance to this institution as psychiatric disorders are seen to a lesser extent in joint families. This low prevalence is usually in comparison to nuclear families. Our personal and clinical impression of joint families in Calcutta has been at variance with this idealised picture. From the very inception of this study, it was intended to examine in depth the various aspects of family life which affect mental health so profoundly.

The first problem that had to be resolved was that of the definition of joint family; not only do the sociological definitions vary greatly, but the family members themselves frequently give contradictory and misleading information about the family structure. The economic definition adopted by us finally eliminated the subjective bias (or the formal answers) of the family members and brought the classification in line with the well known one of Conklin's (1968). The results showed that joint families indeed had low prevalence rates for most disorders and nuclear families showed high rates, but the third type of family—extended—emerged with the highest rates of disorders. Extended family or transitional family, as defined by Conklin (1968), is a nuclear family together with various single relations. So, it logically followed that these 'additional' relations constituted the vulnerable group which produced the high rates. To isolate these presumably sick persons, it was necessary to determine their family roles, hence it was imperative to identify the 'index' person or the 'head' of the family.

The 'head' of the family is an emotive term in Bengali culture, mostly expressed in English. It denotes seniority, prestige and status as of 'old days', but present-day realities are often entirely different. We frequently observed that the person bringing in the highest earnings dominated the family. If he was also the seniormost, then the situation was ideal; but in many instances involving father and son, such an ideal situation did not exist. An old or retired father who did not own any property would have no 'power' in the family. But family members would be loath to admit as much to an outsider, and a father would always be designated as the 'head'. In such situations, only an in-depth anthropological study could determine how decision-making, the other most important function of the 'head' besides earning, took place. We did not attempt to go into this complex problem and followed the simpler and probably more authentic criterion (i.e., the economic one) to determine the type of the family (as detailed earlier) and consequently the 'head' of the family. By this measure, the seniormost earning member became the 'head' and all other members of the family were identified according to their relationship to this 'head'. Following the economic criteria, family members were classified as dependent and independent members, that is, those who were holding employment or had sources of income and others who did not contribute to household expenses. Full information on these aspects was collected for the main study.

Conklin (1968) classified Indian families as follows:

I   Nuclear—Father + mother + unmarried children.
II   Transitional—Father + mother + children + assorted single relations.
III   Joint—Two or more related couples, including children and other related persons.
IV   Sub-nuclear—Uni-member family and those nuclear families where one parent was absent.

The uni-member families or unitary households were studied separately (See People living alone). One parent families were also studied, but only where the mother was the 'head' ('female head').

In the present study of family roles, there was a departure from our main study. Non-Bengali families were excluded. Since the researchers and investigators had a better conception of the relationships and family constellations among the Bengalis than the others, it was felt that they would be on firm ground, when required to interpret the questions of rights and obligations of the role relationships among the former.

In the following chart of the 31 types of family roles, the categorisation of (economically) dependent and independent members has been made with actual evidence of employment, etc. But there were also some tacit assumptions or understanding of Bengali family obligations. For instance, if the father was alive and working, grown-up sons and daughters (both married and unmarried) were not considered as dependent. However, in some instances, married daughters were living in their parental home, because they were either widowed or had been abandoned by their husbands. Such daughters were considered to be dependent. Some women lived with their brother who was the 'head' for similar reasons. Some of them were dependent, while others were not, having an independent source of income. Many distant relatives often lived with the index family because of housing difficulties; students lived with relatives because they were studying in Calcutta, etc. Hence, the presence of 'odd' kin in a family did not always indicate a distressing situation.

It should be noted that the families under study were all verilocal, that is, all the designated members were residing at one place and sharing meals (at least 30 meals a month) prepared in the same kitchen. The list of roles included only adult members of the household; children under 14 were not taken into account. In the present chapter, only psychoneuroses and not total morbidity have been considered against each role type.

Following categories of relations were also present in different families, their number and the percentages of neuroses among them were small: Head's—son's daughter, grand father/mother, uncle, daughter's husband/son/daughter, sister's husband/son/daughter, father-in-law, wife's brother's wife.

Note: The criteria for diagnosis of neuroses on which percentages were based were the same as those used in all previous analyses. But neurotic scores have not been used before. Neurotic scores were calculated by adding up the positive answers in the self-report. The scale varied from 1 to 13, with one point each for sleep disturbance and somatic symptoms (at least three). The neurotic score gave indication of the actual complaints, which the diagnosis did not because it was often influenced by facts obtained from other sources, such as relative's corroboration, leisure activities, and disruption of work/studies.

TABLE 5.1
Family Roles, Dependency and Neuroses
(Means are not calculated where the numbers were small: Adults only)

Roles by Definition: Independent

Roles	Total Numbers	Percentages of Neuroses	Mean Neuroses Score
Head—Male	1368	9.9	4.8
Head—Female	72	35.2	7.0
Head's Wife	1228	21.5	5.1
Head's Husband	4	—	—

Roles of Both Categories: Dependent and Independent

Roles		Total Numbers	Percentages of Neuroses	Mean Neuroses Score
Head's				
Son	Independent	923	6.1	4.2
	Dependent	—	—	—
Son's Wife	Independent	106	10.3	4.8
	Dependent	—	—	—
Son's Daughter	Independent	1	—	—
	Dependent	—	—	—
Daughter	Independent	539	8.7	4.3
	Dependent	21	23.8	6.6
Father	Independent	6	—	—
	Dependent	92	20.6	5.0
Mother	Independent	16	25.0	5.0
	Dependent	369	28.9	5.7
Aunt	Independent	—	—	—
	Dependent	22	18.1	4.8
Brother	Independent	358	7.2	5.0
	Dependent	121	12.3	4.6
Brother's Wife	Independent	96	13.5	5.1
	Dependent	12	41.6	5.8
Brother's Son	Independent	30	6.6	4.8
	Dependent	14	14.2	—
Brother's Daughter	Independent	20	20.0	—
	Dependent	11	—	—

Table 5.1 (Contd.)

Roles		Total Numbers	Percentages of Neuroses	Mean Neuroses Score
Sister	Independent	62	12.9	4.8
	Dependent	179	15.0	5.1
Mother-in-law	Independent	1	—	—
	Dependent	22	50.0	6.6
Relative (Distant)	Independent	55	14.5	6.4
	Dependent	17	17.6	5.5
Wife's Brother	Independent	11	18.1	—
	Dependent	7	28.5	—

TABLE 5.2
Significance of Economic Dependency in Neuroses

(a)		Number	Psycho-neuroses	Rate (Per cent)
Grade I	Members by Definition Independent	3712	491	13.2
	Other Members Excluding Above	2149	319	13.8
	df1 X²	2.99		NS

(b) Members Belonging to Either Category

		Number	Psycho-neuroses	Rate (Per cent)
Grade II	Independent Members (Excluding Grade I)	1234	115	9.3
Grade III	Dependent Members	915	204	22.2
	df1 X²	69.94		p.<.0001

(c) Distribution of Grade II and III Members by Family Type

	Nuclear	Extended	Joint
Independent Members	20.0	6.1	73.8
Dependent Members	1.3	40.4	58.2

Interpretation

The differences in dealing with sons and daughters did not affect the calculations. It so happened that a few married or widowed daughters were actually dependent on the 'head', whereas none of the married sons in this sample were.

As far as roles are concerned, it was seen that the female 'head' was under maximum stress. The head's wife also showed high rates and high scores, but these roles, self-evidently, faced quite different types of stresses than others. In all other role types, dependent members had much higher rates than independent members, a finding which is highly significant. However, it was not financial distress alone that made some role types more vulnerable, the implication of dependent status varied according to the relationship. For instance, dependent daughters suffered more than dependent sisters. In fact, the better mental health of sisters and their families seemed to support the popular notion that maternal uncle's house (*mama-bari*) always denoted love, affection and care. In contrast, brothers, even when they were independent, had more than their share of neuroses. Brothers' wives (dependents) had the second highest rate and it is probable that rivalry played a part in this relationship. Mothers-in-law, understandably, were highly distressed to be dependent on their sons-in-law. On the other hand, mothers, whether dependent or independent, had almost similar high rates, which was probably a reflection of age. It was not clear why relatives (mostly females) even when they were independent had such high scores. It may be possible that the feeling of being 'outsiders', and not having their own families deprived them of status and self-esteem.

It is seen (Table 5.2c) that extended families had a high proportion of dependent members (though less than those in joint families), whose presence presumably caused more stresses, because there was only one earning member in such families, in contrast to joint families where there were at least two earning members. It is very likely that such stresses were causal in producing significantly high rates of neuroses in extended families and among the dependent members.

Discussion

There is no agreement among Indian sociologists about the nature and structure of Indian families. Popular notions and myths tend to generalise and present a glorified image of Indian families, as if these were immutable entities, unaltered over time and place. It is believed that all Indian families were initially large joint families based in villages which, with industrialisation, moved into cities and broke up into small nuclear families. These ideas have been challenged on the strength of actual investigations. A.M. Shah (1973), one of the leading sociologists in India, believes that the idealised notions of patrilinear, patrilocal joint families are products of Hindu upper caste strictures on funeral rites (*Sradh*). Among upper caste Hindus, a son is primarily valued because he will light the funeral pyre and perform the complicated ceremonies on the death of his parents and, if required, for other patrilinear relatives. However, such types of families had never been the norm among the different castes in India. Also, the other unsupported idea about the 'breaking up' of agricultural communities in the villages is equally untrue. Migration has always occurred, with artisans often moving from one place and settling in other places. There had been cities in India even in mythical times! Shah (1973) has maintained that families are often in a flux, they break up in one place and form in another. For example, if one member of a family goes to the city, the other members gradually join him there, forming new joint families. There are numerous factors which influence these groupings and re-groupings of family members.

Indian psychiatrists have mostly taken the aforesaid idealistic view of families. Joint families have always shown lower rates of morbidity (Sethi *et al.*, 1967, 1974; Verghese *et al.*, 1973) as seen in our study. Such findings have been used to extol the virtues of joint families. Sethi and Manchanda (1978a and b) have even observed an 'in-built mechanism' which prevents mental disorders. Indian studies have used the Khatri scale of jointness; but, as these authors have pointed out, most studies ultimately use a division between nuclear and joint, where the presence of any relative in a nuclear family made it joint. Though Sethi and Manchanda have not clarified what the beneficial mechanism was in the joint family, the implicit idea was perhaps (*a*) the elderly were looked after, (*b*) the elderly looked after the sick, and (*c*) mutual support of joint families prevented sickness from becoming manifest.

We agree that the rates of sickness in joint families are usually less than in other types of families, but we offer other explanations for it. Before proceeding further, it should be stated that we fully agree that nuclear families seem to harbour considerable stress, and that a high level of sickness is found among them. Our data supported these notions. However, we differ with regard to the so-called 'altruistic mechanism' through which joint families are supposed to maintain their good health.

It is postulated that

1. Joint families have either continued for a long time, or they have recently been formed by the grouping of two or more financially solvent persons.
2. Such families often exclude sick persons, or the weaker section of the family.
3. Such families are not required to look after their elderly dependents or young wives.

It is conjectured that the process in the formation of joint families may be as follows. The father dies, the mother and younger children continue to stay in the same place, the older son may be already working elsewhere, where he is joined by another working brother. In the original household one of the younger sons gets a job, but continues to stay with the mother. An aunt or a widowed sister may have been living there, or may move in, because being the ancestral home, they have some rights. The family members who stay away will maintain good relations and help the original household financially. Yet another process may take place, that is, a mother-in-law (or other such person) without any means of livelihood is likely to live with the nuclear family of the son-in-law, than join the unit in which he is staying with his parents or brothers.

On the whole, there were many indications that joint families were formed or remained so, when and where the circumstances so permitted. Earlier it was seen that joint families had a high adults to children ratio (3:1). This implied that mothers of young children who were likely to be most stressed were in fewer numbers in joint families. Whether because of this fact or due to other reasons, the number of retarded and epileptics was fewer in joint families (see Table 4.3). It seems unlikely that this was because the elderly relatives gave more attention to pregnant mothers, because such attention should have been seen in extended families as well and would presumably be absent in nuclear families, but the overall rates of retardation and epilepsy were only marginally different in these two types of families, with the rates in nuclear families being slightly higher (Table 4.3). Further, it was found that apart from mild retardation, all other disorders were more common in extended families, far more than their proportion in the total distribution of families (Table 5.3). The incidence of both psychoses and psychoneuroses was higher in extended families, and the association of psychoneuroses was statistically significant (Table 4.14a). It is not surprising to find a high level of neuroses in extended families, because persons with dependent status, which proved to be very stressful, were seen in large numbers in such families, but the high rates of other disorders in these families could not be explained. The presence of sick members probably facilitates the 'break-up' of joint families, or a regrouping takes place with one member accepting the responsibility of the sick person.

Joint families also seemed to be less burdened by economically dependent elderly people, especially females (see section on old people). So, it seems that the very structure which allows no scope for vulnerable people to be included, that is, a kind of positive selection, is the mechanism by which joint families ensured their mental health. However, variables, such as, social class in relation to age and sex and other similar aspects, need to be thoroughly probed before the beneficial effects of joint living can really be ascertained.

We believe that our conclusion that joint families maintain their good mental health by a process of exclusion and selection is justified. However, it must be emphasised that this was seen in families in Calcutta at a definite period of time. It must be noted that the conclusions could not be generalised to all Indian communities, which are noted for their extreme diversity. Further, the developmental process in families, either progression or regression, affects the relationships of a person with other members of the household and hence, the various situations in which the role relationships are enacted have to be taken into account (Shah, 1973) in order to understand the stresses generated.

There is no denying of the fact that when joint families function smoothly, they offer tremendous support. According to Sandel (1982),

Middle and lower status respondents from nuclear families most commonly reported feelings of anxiety at the lack of an older person in the house. Older women seemed to provide a sense of reassurance and act as confidantes and advisers to younger wives, since very few even in the upper 'liberated' classes saw marriage and the husband as providing support of this sort. This is so common as to be part of the culturally determined set of expectations of the roles within a marriage rather than a manifestation of poor marital relationships. That older family members fulfil this role in a joint family, is seen in the statements of both men and women often well into their late middle age of feeling bereft at the death of father, mother or older sibling.

TABLE 5.3
Distribution of the Sampled Persons and Disorders by Family Types

Family Type	Nuclear	Extended	Joint	Unitary	Total
All Persons	4426	1806	6740	363	13335
Row (per cent)	33.1	13.5	50.5	2.7	100.0
All Disorders	519	294	790	56	1659
Row (per cent)	31.1	17.7	47.6	3.3	100.0

PEOPLE LIVING ALONE OR IN HOSTELS AND 'HOMES'

Ever since the classical study of the 1920s by Faris and Dunham (1960) revealed high rates of schizophrenia in socially disorganised city areas, living alone without a family or without a 'fixed abode' has become suspect. Whether the high morbidity seen among such people is the result of loneliness, insecurity and city bred alienation, or whether it is a result of innate maladjustments which make mentally ill people prefer to live alone is a controversial issue.

Migration into the cities from rural areas and the consequent rootlessness stemming from the inability to create a home and have a family because of an indifferent and discouraging environment—urbanisation—have also added to the stresses of living alone. Homelessness affects women and children through death or desertion on the part of the husband and father. Such broken home families are known to generate morbidity and misery.

Studying solitary people is difficult even in a field survey as they tend to move away frequently. The sampling has to be very stringent to bring such people within the parameters of population distribution. We were fortunate that a team from the Indian Statistical Institute, which specialised in population studies, did the sampling as well as the first stage stratification and identification.

The entire study on the mental health of the population in Calcutta was based on families as units; the special group under discussion was categorised as single-member families or unitary households. Many similar surveys have been criticised because the definitions of 'family' or 'household' were made so rigid that unitary households—a most vulnerable section of the population—were excluded (Gruenberg, 1965).

Demographic Features

Unitary households—363, 14.4 per cent of the total number of households, 2512; or 2.7 per cent of the sampled persons, 13335.

Number of persons living in homes—18.7 per cent; hostels—10.4 per cent; separate establishments—70.7 per cent.

Language groups—Bengalis, 43.2 per cent; non-Bengalis, 56.7 per cent.

Males–71 per cent, females–28.9 per cent.

TABLE 5.4a
People Living Alone—Age Groups

Years	Male (Per cent)	Female (Per cent)
0–13	—	15.2
14–24	22.0	39.0
25–39	39.7	10.4
40–49	18.6	6.6
50–59	13.5	12.3
60+	6.2	16.1
	100.0	100.0

TABLE 5.4b
People Living Alone—Occupations

	Male (Per cent)	Female (Per cent)
Students	6.5	20.0
Non-earners	3.8	22.8
Low Occupation	34.4	20.9
Middle Occupation	36.8	18.0
High Occupation	18.2	18.0
	100.0	100.0

TABLE 5.4c
People Living Alone—Religious Groups

	Per cent	*In total sample (Per cent)*
Hindu	80.4	90.0
Muslim	9.9	7.2
Christian	6.6	1.3
Others	3.0	1.3
	100.0	100.0

TABLE 5.5
Comparison of Disorders Between Unitary Households and Others
(in per cent)

	Unitary Households	*Others*
Mental Retardation and Epilepsy	1.9	2.0
Abnormal Personality and Paranoid States	0.8	1.2
Psychoses	0.2	0.7
Possession State and *Suchi-bai*	2.3	2.2
Neuroses	10.6	10.9

There were six mildly retarded persons and one epileptic in this group. The retarded were mostly children in an orphanage. There was only one psychotic, who managed to look after herself with help from her neighbours in the slum. It was learnt that her husband would visit her occasionally and leave some money with the neighbours. The two cases of possession state were virtual celebrities in their neighbourhood.

Discussion

From the demographic features it will be seen that the majority were living in their own establishments. They were working men (Table 5.4b) who were mostly migrants (i.e., people who had a family in their native place). This feature is being emphasised to show that, contrary to a common observation in western surveys, in Calcutta the majority of unitary households did not comprise the fringe population of hobos, derelicts and beggars. The Bengali: non-Bengali ratio in the population was 70:30, but in the case of unitary households it was nearly 43:57. In the latter case a few or even most of the non-Bengali migrants did not 'make it' and remained at the poverty level as seen in the economic distribution (see section on Ethnics, Migrants and Religious Groups and Table 5.6b). Some of these people were, no doubt, destitutes, beggars and rag-pickers who had been placed in the low or non-earning groups but, on the whole, the number of extremely poor persons was not found to be high in the unitary households. The point to be noted here is that poverty did not seem to contribute towards the fragmentation of families.

As indicators of social disintegration and stress, the small group of females provided a more accurate picture. It was seen that the age structure of men in this group was fairly close to that of the population, i.e., it was a normal distribution. In the case of women, however, the picture was very different. There were fewer women than men, thereby suggesting that adverse circumstances had forced them to live alone. That 50 per cent of these women were young girls and women who were non-earners, further suggests that they were in homes for protection (Table 5.4b; the designation of students among females only meant school-going young girls).

Most of the women in 'homes' were young girls and women who did not have any relatives, or whose families had broken up. Hostels for men referred to college hostels, but the two working girls' hostels were really 'homes' as they were subsidised and most of the girls only did nominal work. Women with 'high occupations' were nurses, teachers and secretaries. Though some of them lived in hostels, yet most lived separately. A group of six or seven prostitutes we interviewed, gave the most heart rending stories about ill treatment by husbands and broken homes. All of them had some neurotic complaint. With the exception of one 'German Bibi' who was hostile and made caustic remarks, others were willing to talk and expressed a desire to leave their profession.

The other extremely disadvantaged group included elderly women who lived on their own. They numbered more than men and most of them were widows. Though many of them had children, yet for one reason or another they were living separately. It could be possible that after the death of their husbands, their daughters-in-law had an upper hand. The majority of these old Bengali women had complaints, and some of them had severe symptoms.

However, the rates of various disorders were either the same or lower than the sample average. Hence, it could not be said that living alone was particularly stressful.

An interesting feature of these unitary households was that the percentages of religious groups (other than Hindus) were higher than those in the entire sample (Table 5.4c), the difference being highest among Christians. Though the sample was too small to justify any definite conclusion, yet we could suggest that social disruption and consequent homelessness had affected the other religious communities more than the Hindus.

These indicators strengthened our impression that, despite overwhelming poverty, social disintegration (as exemplified by broken families) was not seen among the Bengalis in greater Calcutta. The number of broken families was small and an isolated phenomenon.

Samples of conversation with some people living alone are cited here to throw some light on their lives.

MEN STUDENTS IN HOSTELS

One well-known politician's brother from another state said, 'I take liquor, *ganja*, LSD, everything. You can write it down.' One person complained of nervousness and palpitation, and another of restlessness. A boy who had dropped out of the engineering course because of ragging complained of 'the same thought' coming to his mind all the time and of depression.

A man, 50 years. A beggar who was almost blind. He complained only of pain due to hydrocele.

A man, 50 years. A jute mill worker with good earnings, said, 'I am quite well now, my head is no longer hot.' (A friend next door reported that he drank heavily, threatened people with knives and talked incessantly at times.)

A young man, 24 years. A Muslim, who complained of all the symptoms in our schedule and added a few more, all these symptoms had persisted since the last 6 to 7 years. When asked whether there was a reason for his complaints he replied, 'you don't need to know the reasons'!

A Muslim tailor, 37 years. Used to have fits earlier, but now they occurred only when he had fever. His family lived in a village far away. He complained of extreme worries, fear of falling down on the street and a feeling 'as if there was somebody behind' all the time.

There were several old men and jute mill workers who had no complaints. Most men either had health problems or sought advice on health related matters. Most of the Bengalis in unitary households had families living in nearby villages or towns.

Girls in the orphanage were rather unhappy and subdued, and had nothing much to say. A young child aged 9 years narrated how her uncle killed her father 'for the house' (the local superintendent added that the child's mother, severely depressed, was staying with her brothers). Another girl (14 years), an inmate of the same orphanage, complained of severe burning of the head which would lead to unconsciousness especially when she went home for a visit.

One working women's hostel had several Anglo-Indian girls, some of them had good jobs. They were happy and carefree. A few of them were 'students'.

In one subsidised hostel, a girl (19 years) repeatedly asked, 'Tell me, what will happen to me?' She said that she would like to get a job, but the only job she was doing now was to steal. Others forced her to steal food from the hostel kitchen.

Many nurses and secretaries living alone had severe health problems including heart problems, etc. A woman employed as an ayah in a hospital was lying naked in bed when we visited her. She seemed to be unconcerned and did not make an effort to put on any clothes. She talked, but was irritable and hostile. She was known not to talk to anybody, including patients under her care.

ETHNICS, MIGRANTS AND RELIGIOUS GROUPS

Persons whose mother tongue was not Bengali comprised a large minority in Calcutta and its surrounding areas. They have been referred to as non-Bengalis or migrants. There were several ethnic groups speaking different languages, as well as different types of migrants and 'refugees'.

Broadly speaking, there were non-Bengali families who had been living in Calcutta for at least three generations, and they were totally assimilated, though they continued to maintain their separate identity. These people were found either in very rich business communities or among very poor labourers, service workers or menials. Then there were those who had transferable jobs and were posted in Calcutta, as well as poor people from other states who had come to Calcutta in search of work or business. Only this latter group was composed of true migrants (internal), the other migrants being Bengali-speaking people from surrounding villages in search of work. A section of these people usually returned to their villages, and hence these seasonal migrants have not been covered in the present survey. Another group settled down in the suburbs, keeping close contact with their native village.

Then there were the 'refugees'. Following the partition of the country and Independence, there was a massive influx of refugees from East Pakistan. These people were totally assimilated and no longer had separate identities, except in a rather subtle form (Chakraborty, 1978a). After Independence many non-Bengali (for example, Punjabi-speaking) refugees had also settled in Calcutta.

There were other groups, though small in number, yet no less important, such as Urdu-speaking Muslims and English-speaking Anglo-Indians. They belonged to Calcutta, having no other home state, but their identities were distinct from that of Bengalis.

The following analysis and discussions focus on all non-Bengali-speaking minorities grouped together. Bengali-speaking 'refugees' and migrants have not been included except in passing.

SAMPLE SIZE: 13335. Bengalis—71.1 per cent,
non-Bengalis—28.8 per cent.

TABLE 5.6a
Male–Female Ratio in Different Age Groups Among Ethnic Groups

Age Groups	−13	−24	−39	−49	−59	60+
Bengalis	1.01	1.07	1.12	1.29	1.39	0.92
Non-Bengalis	1.1	1.49	1.57	2.0	2.4	1.38

TABLE 5.6b
Economic Strata Distribution Among Ethnic Groups

	Low Economic Strata		Middle Economic Strata		High Economic Strata	
Bengalis	20.0		60.7		19.2	—	100.0
		69.7		71.9		66.7	
Non-Bengalis	20.7		56.4		22.7	—	100.0
		30.2		28.0		33.2	
		100.0		100.0		100.0	

We can see that nearly one-third of greater Calcutta's population was composed of different ethnic groups, other than the Bengali majority. The male:female ratio among non-Bengalis was more in favour of males than that seen in the case of Bengalis. Though the proportion of poor people was the same, the proportion of affluent people was higher among the ethnic groups. Bengalis, both males and females, were better educated and, consequently, had higher status in occupation.

Somatisation and Language

The neuroses questionnaire (IRS) was expected to produce problems in detecting subjective distress among the ethnic groups as their members spoke different languages (though the majority spoke Hindi). To overcome this difficulty emphasis was laid on somatisation, which was taken to denote the expression of psychological distress through physical complaints. Accepting the prevalent idea that somatisation occurs because of poor verbal abilities, we expected that if there were constraints on account of language, it would produce more somatisation. There was also a tacit assumption that Bengali being a highly developed language and Bengalis being extremely vocal, they would somatise less than non-Bengalis.

However, all these assumptions were belied, as language posed no problems—Hindi or English, in addition to Bengali were understood by all the respondents. Also, Bengalis somatised no less than others as seen in Table 5.7.

TABLE 5.7
Somatic Complaints by Sex and Ethnic Groups

Somatic Complaints	Females Bengali/Non-Bengali		Males Bengali/Non-Bengali		
Aches and Pains	54.9	11.7	21.6	10.6	100%
Burning Sensations	56.5	14.0	21.0	8.3	100%
Stomach Trouble	43.4	9.1	36.2	11.1	100%
Headache	55.1	12.7	25.2	6.8	100%
Weakness	48.3	12.3	28.4	10.8	100%
Palpitation	59.4	11.0	21.8	7.6	100%
Sleep Problems	48.2	10.0	32.5	9.1	100%

It appeared that somatisation was more frequent among females. Bengali women were somatisers *par excellence* and neuroses were also common among them. These two features were found to be closely related (Chakraborty and Sandel, 1985).

TABLE 5.8
Comparison of Disorders Among Ethnic Groups
(Bengalis vs. Non-Bengalis)

	Rates/1000 Non-Bengali Population	Rates/1000 Bengali Population
All Persons		
Severe Mental Retardation	2.6	4.3
Mild Mental Retardation	5.2	13.1
Epilepsy	6.2	5.7
	14.0	23.1
Adults Only		
Possession State	3.9	4.8
Suchi-bai	6.2	22.3
Paranoid State	1.1	5.1
Abnormal Personality	6.2	8.7
Disturbed Psychosis	2.3	2.5
Quiet Psychosis	3.1	3.5
Depressed Psychosis	1.1	1.6
Psychoneuroses	68.6	125.7
	92.5	174.2

The large difference in the overall rates was mainly produced by the neuroses categories, but a few others deserve discussion.

The low rate of severe retardation among the ethnics may have been due to the reason stated earlier, i.e., benign neglect, and this probably was more common among the poorly educated labourers. The low rate of mild retardation may also have been due to the poor perception on the parents' part of the intellectual development of their children. Aspirations and expectations, known to add a dimension to mild retardation (Stein and Susser, 1975), could have been different among them.

Psychoses rates were the same, whereas the rate for abnormal personality was not very different, but paranoid conditions were much less frequent among non-Bengalis. The reason could very well have been concealment. If they were paranoid about Bengalis, naturally it could not be talked about! Even otherwise, on an individual level, this information may not have been disclosed by other family members. (This item was included in the Family Report which obtained information from a key relative.) However, it is difficult to say that concealment was the sole reason for the difference in the rates, particularly when psychoses were readily revealed.

Suchi-bai or pollution mania was not unknown among the ethnics. It was seen in sizeable numbers, though not to the same extent as among Bengalis.

Possession state, well-known for its occurrence all over India, was found to a similar extent among the two communities.

As has been noted earlier, psychoneuroses rates were found to be much lower among non-Bengalis. The reasons for this low rate could be the following:

1. The instrument for detecting neuroses was not sufficiently sensitive in the case of ethnic groups.
2. The difference was mainly due to differences in the demographic features. The ethnic groups included a smaller number of women and old people and hence, they showed a low rate for the disorder which was more common among females and old people. Conversely, working men, who rarely suffer from psychoneuroses, were comparatively numerous among the ethnics.
3. The personality characteristics and expectations were different between the two groups. The Bengalis talked more and demanded help, whereas talking about themselves was rather alien to most of the ethnic groups (particularly in the case of the migrants), who also expected little outside help.
4. Genuine lower occurrence of neuroses among people other than Bengalis.

Though it is not denied that the first three were equally important and contributory factors, it was our impression that the low occurrence of psychoneuroses, in absolute terms, among some of the ethnic groups did account for the low morbidity. This conclusion was supported by the low level of somatisation and hysteria, which was 50 per cent lower than that among the Bengalis. The significance of this fact is that the ethnic groups had lower levels of literacy than the

Bengalis and these two conditions are usually associated with education.

Other aspects of personality and social background of the Bengalis and other groups are presented in Table 5.9.

TABLE 5.9
Social and Personality Problems

	Rates/1000 Bengalis	Rates/1000 Non-Bengalis
Irritability	15.0	12.2
Gross Personality Disorders	8.7	6.2
Anti-social Acts	3.3	2.3
Alcohol Consumption	15.0	60.8
Drug Taking	2.8	14.0

In terms of the categories which give rise to social problems, the two groups were not very different. But as far as alcohol and drug consumption were concerned, the ethnic groups surpassed the Bengalis. Again, this was due to the demographic differences. The problems mentioned were more common among men; in addition, alcohol and drug use were predominant in the two occupational groups—mill workers and scavengers (that is, garbage collectors). These occupations were almost entirely confined to certain ethnic and migrant groups.

Since alcoholism is a well known affliction among workers all over the world, the present figures may not signify poor mental health among ethnic and migrant workers in Calcutta.

Conclusion

The assessment of the mental health status of such a huge and diverse 'minority' by representatives of the majority community naturally raises the question of reliability, over and above all the pitfalls that are inherent in field surveys. We were aware of these problems and separate assessments were made for candour, co-operation and friendliness of the neighbourhood. These assessments revealed that un-cooperativeness was seen among 3 per cent of the families, while 4 per cent of the families reported their neighbourhood to be unfriendly. Though these negative feelings were higher among the ethnic groups, the percentages were low. There was no reason to believe that information was being suppressed, particularly at the lower levels. However, this was not entirely true as very rich trading communities had been deliberately misleading. These people often lived in large joint families with very orthodox life-styles, and they did not like outsiders asking them intimate questions. Fortunately such families were very few in number.

In terms of the overall figures, both ethnic and migrant groups had almost similar mental health problems as the locals, except in the case of psychoneuroses which were lower among these groups (particularly for stress related conditions, such as, anxiety and depression; Chakraborty, 1985). Several reasons have been given to account for this difference. Assuming the differences to be true, there is yet another possibility. The figures given are comparative: instead of saying that the ethnic groups were less vulnerable, it may be said that the locals were more so. Bengali women, it seemed, were particularly prone to psychoneuroses. It may be recalled that neuroses rates in other parts of India were found to be much lower (see discussion under morbidity rates).

It can be safely concluded that ethnic and migrant groups in Calcutta did not have any worse mental health than the locals. In other words, they were not subjected to any additional stress on account of having to live in an alien climate. However, this conclusion is at variance with the findings of two other studies of internal migrants in India. Bhaskaran *et al.* (1970) in Ranchi and Sethi *et al.* (1972) in Lucknow reported that migrant industrial workers and their families had high rates of morbidity. The fact that migrant or ethnic groups in Calcutta did not show increased vulnerability may be due to their inherent better health, or that they appeared to be more healthy simply because the local population was unhealthy. This aspect of comparison between locals and migrants has been repeatedly pointed out by Murphy (1977).

It may be possible that the migrant groups as opposed to the settled ethnic groups were subjected to different types of stresses which got masked by considering them together. It is a well known fact that when 'out-groups' have large communities of their own they have less adjustment problems. In Calcutta, most communities have their own schools and shops and entertainment halls, they live along with the local population and there are practically no ghettos. In addition, overt or covert pressures to conform to any particular life-style or cultural mores are absent. These characteristics of Calcutta must be taken into account when studying ethnic problems. Such studies do not seem to have been conducted in India as yet.

Religion, Ethnic Groups and Mental Disorders

It will not be out of place to introduce religious groups here, since religions in India often follow ethnic lines. Table 5.10 is self-explanatory. (All the disorders have been considered together. 'Other' signifies Sikhs, Jains, Buddhists, etc.)

TABLE 5.10
Overall Disorder Rates Among Ethnic and Religious Groups

		Affected Persons (in Per cent)	Per cent Affected Within Group
Hindu Bengali	67	79	15.7
Hindu Non-Bengali	22	13.4	7.9
Muslim Bengali	2.7	2.5	12.0
Muslim Non-Bengali	4.4	2.7	8.4
Christian Bengali	0.65	0.83	17.2
Christian Non-Bengali	0.68	0.61	11.9
Other Bengali	0.26	0.16	8.5
Other Non-Bengali	1.1	0.5	4.5
Total (13335)	100	100	

The table shows that Bengalis of whatever religion had the highest rates. Christians also appeared to be at risk, both Bengali Christians as well as non-Bengali Christians. There was no indication to suggest that they felt persecuted, though after Independence they had lost much of their position and privileges. Many Christian girls lived in hostels, and those living alone gave histories of broken families through migration abroad, etc.

In terms of religion too, Calcutta showed a great deal of tolerance and compassion, not withstanding the fact that Hindu-Muslim riots had taken place in Calcutta in the past.

PROBLEMS OF OLD AGE

Disorders and demographic features pertaining to all persons belonging to the 60 years and above age group have been compiled in the main tables. However, a special section giving further details and highlighting the different problems of old age was considered necessary. Geriatric problems are relatively new in Indian society, and as yet of far lesser magnitude than in the west, but these can no longer be overlooked.

Demographic Features

The number of persons in the age group of 60 years and above are 5.9 per cent of the population (1971 Census—5.3 per cent)

The group consisted of 786 people or 8.6 per cent of the total sample.

Male-female ratio came down from 1.6:1 in the 50 to 59 years age group, to 1: 1 in the 60 years and above age group.

TABLE 5.11
Marital Status Among Higher Age Groups

		Single	Married	Widow/Widower
Male				
50–59 years	(561)	4.8	91.6	3.5
60+ years	(394)	5.5	81.7	12.6
Female				
50–59 years	(348)	2.8	58.6	38.5
60+ years	(392)	2.0	26.5	71.4

The major demographic changes found in the over 60 years age group, particularly among females, were probably due to the return of the migrant workers to their native place, which equalised the male:female ratio. The large age difference between a man and his wife, so common in Indian communities, probably accounted for the disproportionately high percentage of widows, as the elderly husbands were likely to have died before their wives.

There were proportionately more old people in the upper economic strata than in the lower strata.

It was observed that 57 per cent of the old people had poor education, in contrast to 40 per cent in the 50–59 years age group.

Only 20 per cent of the old people were employed in some gainful occupation, or were earning.

About 58 per cent of the old people were living in joint families, and 25 per cent in extended families. The proportions of persons living in joint families and extended families in the population were 50 per cent and 13 per cent respectively (Table 5.3).

More women were living in extended families, which indicated that more women than men became financially dependent on their relatives in old age.

The rate for psychoneuroses was highest in the over 60s age group both for males and females. Depressive psychosis was also highest in this age group, as was psychosis with disturbed behaviour among males.

Disorders of Memory

As stated earlier, definite criteria to detect memory disorder were not adopted. More reliance was placed on cultural perception and identification by the vernacular term denoting senility.

The severity of dementia was detected indirectly. All adult persons were given the IRS (self-report) to detect neuroses; on the basis of the responses and the comments of the field investigators, some of these self-reports were rejected as unreliable. Persons who were identified as dementia by the Family Report, and whose self-reports were unreliable, were considered severe cases. Those who were identified as dementia, but could comprehend the questions included in the self-report and answer fairly coherently, were considered mild cases. Some of these latter cases had somatic and neurotic complaints, as well as sleep disturbances.

The following demographic break-up includes all the cases where memory disorders were observed. Some conditions, like alcoholism, *suchi-bai*, as well as neuroses remain as overlapping categories.

TABLE 5.12
Demographic and Other Variables in Memory Disorders
(Percentages are of the number of persons in that particular group)

		Total	Cases	(Percentage)
Sex	Male	394	21	(5.3)
	Female	392	44	(11.2)
Marital	Single	30	2	(6.6)
Status	Married	426	23	(5.3)
	Widow/Widower	330	40	(12.1)
Education	Low	452	56	(12.3)
	Middle	167	9	(5.3)
	High	167	0	(–)
Economic	Low	125	21	(16.8)
Strata	Middle	453	27	(5.9)
	High	208	17	(8.1)
Family Type	Nuclear	91	2	(2.1)
	Extended	197	20	(10.1)
	Joint	455	38	(8.3)
	Single	44	5	(11.3)
Language Group	Bengali	561	56	(9.9)
	Others	225	9	(4.0)
Location	Calcutta	401	32	(7.9)
	Outside Calcutta	281	22	(.7.8)
	Villages	51	4	(7.8)
	Slums	53	7	(13.2)

TABLE 5.13
Rates of Disorders Among Higher Age Groups (60 years and over)

Number of Persons with Memory Disorders:	0.7 per cent of the adult population
	8.2 per cent of the 60+ age group

All Psychiatric Disorders:	*Age Specific Rate per 1000*
Retardation and Epilepsy	7.6
Psychoses and Related Disorders	26.7
Psychoneuroses	195.9
	230.2
Severe Memory Disorders	41.9
	272.1
Mild Memory Disorders	40.7
	312.8

In a community study of people of over 50 years of age in a small town near Madras, Ramchandran *et al.* (1979) found age-specific rates of 32/1000 and 318/1000 for organic and functional disorders respectively. The overall rate of 350/1000 was not very different from that observed in the present study, that is, 312/1000. Even for organic disorders, the rates were well within the comparable range of our rates for severe memory disorders. Ramchandran *et al.* (1979) state that if the lower limits of age had been 65 years in their study, the rates of organic brain disorders would have been 85/1000 (the figure being 82/1000 in our study for the over 60s group). These similarities were noted inspite of the fact that formal medical diagnoses were made for the cases in Madras but not for ours.

All the demographic factors coupled with our findings indicate that older people were at a considerable disadvantage in Calcutta. At a slightly lower age, great disparity was observed in the male:female ratio. This disparity may not have been due only to in-migration of male workers. It has been suggested (Mitra, 1986) that mortality among women was higher in the 40–49 years age group. Men seemed to have higher mortality above 60 years of age. In West Bengal, life expectancy has not increased to any appreciable extent as the proportion of the over-60s age group has remained constant at 6 per cent of the population over the last 20 years (Mitra 1986). The affluent sections had a higher proportion of older people, which perhaps signified better medical care.

Older people had more mental disorders and the association of these disorders with older age groups was stronger than with other age groups. Subjective distresses in particular were very high, as seen in the figures for neuroses. Though a higher proportion of old people lived in joint families which had lower rates for all disorders, the curious phenomenon of extended families cannot be over-looked. The number of economically dependent old people was disproportionately high in these families and the rates of distress were significantly high. Economic dependency on another person, even on a son, was one of the most important factors producing distress.

Whatever the statistics showed, in human terms it was the plight of the old people which aroused the most sympathetic area reports from the investigators of the study. There were areas where most young men could not be contacted for days. They would have gone to pilfer rice from trains entering the 'cordoned areas' (that is, where rationing was in force). Till they returned, the 'old people starved'. How these people survived was a mystery. The most bitter complaints about family affairs were those regarding sons who did not look after their parents. There was hardly a father in this megapolis who had abandoned his family, but there were many sons who had gone away. However, it would be wrong to conclude that all the poor old people were unhappy, or that all the affluent ones were happy. In the most adverse circumstances some carried on like Mother Courage! To illustrate, a few comments made by old people who lived alone, are presented here.

An 85 year old almost blind woman who lived alone said, 'I am fed up with God, what's the use of praying? He does not listen.'

An 80 year old woman lived alone in her own house. Her daughter lived nearby and helped her. She was hard of hearing, but was very talkative. She had obsessional and neurotic complaints, and was also 'forgetful'.

A Muslim beggar woman (78 years) said, 'No one of my family surviving, I worry too much, who will look after me?' She was depressed.

A 72 year old wealthy woman, who owned a house in a posh locality, said: 'Since my husband's death 6 years ago, I cannot sleep, I pace about all night. Every week I telephone my son in London.' She was severely obsessional and depressed.

A 65 year old woman lived alone, her four sons lived nearby and she would have her meals in their houses. She complained of the neighbours' teasing her. She was pleasantly paranoid.

A retired driver of 80, repeatedly said, 'I have nobody, children are there, but they are nobody to me.' He had neurotic complaints, and was depressed.

OCCUPATIONAL GROUPS

'Health surveys have consistently found higher rates of reported illness among housewives than among employed women,' states Nathanson (1980). Unemployment was found to be one of the potent factors in the onset of depressive illness (Brown and Harris, 1978). Occupation, self-evidently, means something very different in the Indian context than in the west. Various aspects of occupation are peculiar to Indian society, such as, caste specificity of certain occupations, derogatory attitude towards manual work and the restrictions imposed on upper class women taking up a job, which have only recently been relaxed. There are many other social, historical and political factors relating to work, which are no doubt changing, and quite rapidly at that.

However, to be out of work or to be unemployed is not such a social disaster in our essentially agricultural society. It goes without saying that the main point of difference between our society and other societies is that conditions of full employment do not exist. People accept unemployment or part-employment as a part of life. It may be difficult for a young man in an urban area to be without a job, and particularly so if the man has a family. But for a woman to have a good job is considered 'lucky'. These are only broad generalisations. Women of the lower strata have always worked, and for the last one or two decades middle class women have also started working. In the early days when women in large numbers started working, misgivings were expressed that work roles would come into conflict with family roles, and that the traditional home bound Indian women would suffer. Working women in India have been studied by sociologists (Kapur, 1970) and considerable information is available on the subject. However, no study seems to have been conducted as yet on psychiatric morbidity apart from our rather tentative one (Bhattacharya and Chakraborty, 1987). In that study of middle class women engaged in teaching and clerical work, we did not find any evidence of neurosis arising out of role conflicts. Though it was difficult to run a household while working, the women under study felt much happier working. However, in another study, Sandel (1982) has reported a slightly higher rate of neurosis among employed women than among housewives. When the types of employment were seen against class differences, it was observed that lower middle class and lower class working women and much higher rates than housewives of the same class. However, in the upper class, the reverse was true.

The extent of neuroses in different occupational groups is presented in Table 5.14.

It can be seen from the table that apart from women in high level occupations and students, all other categories including housewives had similar rates. It was mentioned earlier that uneducated elderly women were the most distressed. Low level occupations were usually held by this group of women and therefore, the finding was not

TABLE 5.14
Occupation, Sex and Psychoneuroses

		Number of Persons	Affected Persons	Percentages
Housework	M	18	1	5.5
	F	2905	500	17.1
Student	M	572	30	5.2
	F	499	40	8.0
Nil/Unclassifiable	M	685	82	11.9
Occupation	F	215	45	20.9
Low level	M	888	48	5.4
Occupation	F	170	36	21.1
Middle level	M	1572	110	7.0
Occupation (Low)	F	99	19	19.1
Middle level	M	1009	54	5.3
Occupation (High)	F	77	13	16.8
High Occupation	M	318	19	5.9
	F	74	1	1.3
		9101	998	

surprising. However, women in high middle level occupations (teachers, etc.) also had high rates, a finding which was unexpected, but consistent with the observations of Sandel (1982). A comparison of the rates of neuroses among housewives and working women (and others) revealed that there was not much difference (Table 5.15).

TABLE 5.15
Comparison of Prevalence of Neuroses Among Housewives and Working Women

Category	Number	Affected	Percentages
Housewife	2905	500	17.1
Working	420	69	16.4
Unclassifiable	215	45	20.9
	635	114	17.9

Chi Sq. test—Not significant
(For nil or unclassifiable occupation see Chapter 3; people categorised as such were beggars, prostitutes, etc., who had high levels of distress.)

One of the most affected (as far as neurosis was concerned) occupational group was that of domestic servants. This 'low level' occupation accounted for 2.57 per cent of all occupations in the initial sample. Nearly 50 per cent of the domestic servants were 'part-time'.

i.e., they lived with their own families in slums close to their place of work; the other 50 per cent 'lived-in' with their employers. A part of the latter group had left their families in their villages, particularly the men from other states; the rest were females who had no families, they were either widowed, divorced or deserted by their husbands. We have explained earlier (see Chapter 2) why the 'living-in' servants were excluded from the sample. They could not be equated with the family members, as their income levels were very different, neither could they be categorised as unitary householders, as their terms and conditions of living varied widely. However, these women came from the same background and faced the same kind of problems as 'lone women' in homes and hostels (see section on People Living Alone). Nearly 44 per cent of these 80 women (computed separately and not with the main study) had neurotic complaints, which meant a rate much higher than that among the other groups. In addition to the usual stresses faced by these women, they were over-worked and exploited, which added to their misery.

Neurosis levels among men in different occupational groups were much lower than those among women, the only exception being nil or very low earner category where the levels were higher as compared to those for other men.

It has already been shown that women who were economically dependent on others were the most distressed. However, the results revealed that employment did not make a difference to women in general, i.e., it did not affect their vulnerability. Housewives were equally distressed, particularly those in the 25–49 years age group in the lower economic strata. We have evidence that only two groups of women were relatively free from neurotic disorders. The first group comprised the comparatively young and unmarried women, the majority of whom were students. The other group comprised well-placed affluent women, particularly those in high level occupations. In the former group, protection by parents and lack of family responsibilities may have played a part in maintaining their good mental health. Women in the second group probably had considerable personality assets to hold highly responsible jobs in this markedly male dominated society which, together with education and affluence, actively produced good mental health. Only satisfying and responsible employment appears to have a beneficial effect, not just any employment.

Both these groups were small. For the vast majority of women, we have no adequate explanation why they suffer.

6

Conclusions

HEALTH OF THE POPULATION

SINCE the basic survey was on health, the health status of the entire sample of 50,000 people was determined. This was done at different periods, to detect seasonal variations in health conditions. A section of the sample was also subjected to laboratory investigations (CMDA—Survey Report, 1983). The actual health examination was done by doctors of the health team and the present data obtained from their records. About 25 per cent of these health records could not be tallied with the mental health records and hence they were eliminated.

Persons rated as 'ill' were those who had a definite disease but were not necessarily febrile or bedridden.

Comparatively more children had some kind of illness. Deficiencies and diseases were much less in the upper economic strata, in the middle strata also they were less as compared to the lower strata. Visible signs of vitamin deficiencies did not invariably tally with reports of indifferent health.

In earlier literature there was an assumption that mental disorders in the tropical countries were to a great extent related to infections, infestations, and diseases. This assumption has been disproved, even in some remote parts of Africa. Beiser *et al.* (1972), for instance, observed few physical diseases accounting for mental disorders among the Serer people. Collis (1967) also found physical factors to be less important in psychiatric disorders among Nigerians.

Nearly 30 per cent of our sample population was not in the best of health; 10 per cent suffered from some deficiency, but no cases were detected where mental health problems could be directly related to

TABLE 6.1a
Conditions of Physical Health—Children

Health Status of Children		Per cent
Good	2175	68.2
Indifferent	932	29.2
Ill	78	2.4
	3185	100.0

TABLE 6.1 (b)
Conditions of Physical Health—Adults

Health Status of Adults		Per cent
Good	4682	67.2
Indifferent	2147	30.9
Ill	177	1.6
	6946	100.0

deficiency diseases of known categories (for example, pellagra). Anxieties directly related to physical illnesses were, of course, present in large numbers. A rate of approximately 4/1000 population was found, in addition to cases where convulsions or unconsciousness were of organic origin. It was quite possible that deficiencies could have produced neurasthenic or anxiety type of symptoms, which perhaps contributed to general neuroses

ATTITUDES AND NEEDS

The main aim of an epidemiological survey is to provide data on the volume and extent of illnesses to health planners who, according to the need evaluated, fix priorities and provide facilities for treatment and prevention. The need for certain services can be said to be related to the extent of the diseases and it is usually accepted that 'case' rates determine 'need'. In psychiatry the equation is not so simple, as it is often not possible to determine who is a 'case' or whether treatment should be instituted. The problem just mentioned applies to non-referred cases, but where help is sought by the person who has problems we are on firmer grounds. Need can be determined by the number seeking relief; but it must be emphasised that all who suffer do not seek help. There is yet another method for determining need which measures the 'social dysfunction' generated by the illness. The Kota study (Carstairs and Kapur, 1976) had devised a scale of 'social dysfunction' in order to measure need for services. But the results obtained in this study are not easily acceptable; the matter remains complex and controversial.

We have tried to ascertain some aspects of this problem, and in keeping with our 'emic' orientation (looking at any phenomena from 'inside' as it were, rather than from 'outside', as observers) the enquiries were made without any preset notions. What we found perhaps, were the attitudes towards utilising the available facilities, both traditional and modern, and also the conditions for which help was sought.

Both the schedules (FRS and IRS) of our enquiry contained questions regarding treatment taken and desired, the facility used, etc., whenever positive answers were obtained for any complaint. In addition, Investigators wrote reports on the reaction of the respondents to these questions.

The following list presents a broad summary of the positive answers.

Treatment Sought by Persons Suffering from Various Disorders:

		Per cent
Of 201 Persons with Delayed Milestones Advice was Sought by	49	24.3
Of 200 Persons with Mental Retardation Advice was Sought by	17	8.5
Of 442 Persons Who did Not do Well in School Advice was Sought by	10	2.2
Of 79 Persons Who had Epilepsy Advice was Sought by	58	73.4
Of 207 Persons Who had Mental Disorders Advice was Sought by	88	42

Advice was sought for other complaints including physical defects by another 79 persons. Total number of persons who sought advice was 301

Of 486 Persons Who had Retardation, Epilepsy or Mental Illness Advice was Sought by 163 Persons or 47 per cent

For the Disorders Listed Above, Advice was Sought from		
Doctors	205	68.1
Healers	88	29.2
Others	8	2.5

Treatment Sought for Various Neurotic Symptoms:

Number who Sought Advice	2447
Number of Persons Who Sought Advice for	
Somatic Complaints	2280
Sleep Disorder	202

Fits	115
Lack of Concentration	10
Worrying too much	6
Nervousness	10
Restlessness	11
Sweating and Suffocation	13
Excessive Cleanliness	1
Ruminative Thoughts	1
Constant Checking	1
Intense Fear of Objects	13
Feeling Depressed	4

(Percentages are not given as there were overlaps)

Advice was Sought from:		(Per cent)
Doctors	2211	90.6
Healers	172	7
Others	57	2.3

These answers, admittedly, were not detailed enough to enable us to draw any firm conclusion, but they do indicate certain broad trends. It was seen that people readily seek help for epilepsy. People also sought help for mental illness, as well as mental retardation, especially in the early years when the child showed delayed milestones. However, even in the case of mental illness, less than half of the affected persons sought treatment, which included that from healers.

The list of complaints, emerging from the neurosis questionnaire, for which help was sought by the respondents, indicated that very few people did so, and also, whatever help was sought was for somatic problems. Purely psychological problems received the least attention, barring insomnia and 'fits' (which were often thought to be due to physical causes). This logic perhaps prompted them to consult doctors, whereas for mental illness where alternate causations (such as, witchcraft) were suspected, healers were consulted. For neurotic complaints even healers were not consulted.

It was assumed that people would question the investigators about treatment facilities, or their opinion of the cases, but this happened only infrequently. An additional question included in the schedules was to be asked whenever any complaint was made—if consultation with a doctor was desired, or if consultations had already taken place—whether further treatment was desired. Answers, for at least psychiatric complaints, were invariably 'no'. People resented this question as they felt there was an implied criticism in it (as if they were neglecting the patient). People on the whole were eager to talk to the doctor (particularly the one accompanying the survey team) for even minor physical ailments, but they did not wish to go elsewhere for treatment. In the case of psychiatric problems, they felt that a lot of money would have to be spent 'for nothing'. Apprehension of added expenditure, as well as a resigned attitude, were seen. Most people knew that treatment at government hospitals was free, but it still meant travelling and expense one way or another.

It was felt that poor, uneducated persons' need for modern medical treatment and management should be carefully evaluated for all illnesses together and not for mental illness separately. The reason is that these people perceive illnesses as something acute and immediate, for which they expect appropriate treatment. Chronic illnesses are something they cannot cope with, and they tend to ignore these as 'incurable'. It was found that treatment for diseases like gastric ulcer, diabetes, and even for problems related to the heart were not followed up. Long standing psychoses fell into this category, and perhaps a higher degree of resignation was associated with it. This attitude is understandable particularly where medical care has been inadequate for long.

It follows that, where physical suffering was tolerated to this extent, psychological suffering would be further discounted. Neurotic complaints did not merit visit to the doctor, and this was not only a question of expense, as these complaints were not negligible even among the affluent section. It may have been due to the attitude.

There was only one kind of condition that could be identified in the present study, where medical intervention could be safely recommended and instituted; and that pertained to long standing disabilities. Intervention in early and acute conditions in Calcutta and the surrounding areas might not have been of high standard, but was found to be available, which is a radical change from the situation, say, a decade or two ago. All large government hospitals have psychiatry units and out-patients' departments (CMDA Report, 1983). In addition, numerous private facilities are available. Between these two extremes, the great majority of patients get a fair amount of treatment.

It may be pointed out that, by all indications, recovery rates in Indian patients after the first attack are high (WHO, 1979) and chronicity rates are low (Murphy and Raman, 1971). The present study confirmed these views in that the prevalence rates of psychoses were found to be lower than expected. Hence, the problem at hand is not very great, granted the parameter delineated.

The trend all over the world is against the building of large mental hospitals and, in keeping with our local tolerant attitudes, we should continue to keep and treat longstanding cases in the community. It is poverty which often drives these people out on the streets. To help families with sick members, some kind of disability pension may be instituted. Though the problems of disbursement and misuse of such monetary benefits may be enormous, yet these should be weighed against hospitalisation costs, which could be worse.

There is another factor which facilitates community treatment of chronic cases in India, and that is the low dosage requirement of drugs. Patients in Calcutta require far lower maintenance dosage of drugs than what is usually recommended (Chakraborty, 1970, 1982). Ethnic variation of drug dosage is, of course, well known. The WHO collaborating centre for psychopharmacology in India at K.E.M. Hospital in Bombay, has been working on this problem under Professor Bagadia (1987) for some time.

We will comment briefly on two other longstanding disabilities—epilepsy and retardation. Epilepsy has received fairly adequate attention in Calcutta, there is good awareness of the condition and most cases are followed up.

Mental retardation has of late become a 'popular' area for voluntary services. Though residential accommodation is inadequate (destitute homes run by the government, Mother Teresa's 'Missionaries of Charity' and similar other homes provide some beds for the abandoned cases), schools and day care centres for the educable types are coming up. As the magnitude of this problem is not very great, there is no reason why it cannot be tackled by voluntary agencies.

To return to an earlier discussion, we have to decide whether awareness should be created among the public that psychological suffering can be alleviated, or, should people with minor disorders be encouraged to seek help. This is an extremely debatable issue, because the only remedy we can offer in such 'cases' is benzodiazepine. On the other hand, awareness that even chronic illnesses can be ameliorated, should certainly be propagated. Treatment of epilepsy at the primary level has been incorporated in the National Mental Health Programme, where its success will convince the villagers of the worth of these measures. However, we have to remain vigilant that such a programme does not degenerate into a pill dispensing one, destroying whatever traditional mechanisms are available for dealing with illnesses. This is, of course, easier said than done. Once intervention starts, it may prove to be an inexorable process, which is probably already in motion. However, we strongly felt that in whatever way 'need' is perceived or measured, it should not result only in demands for hospital beds and finances. Attitudes and orientation of the planners, especially a healthy respect for people's internal resources, may help to avoid some pitfalls that mental health services on a large scale tend to incur.

The area covered by the present study had a radius of about 50 miles around Calcutta, which included eight villages. Problems in the semi-urban hinterland of Calcutta were more acute, and people in these areas availed themselves of the facilities provided by the city to a greater extent than the local inhabitants (CMDA Report, 1983). The villages were in no way representative of villages in West Bengal, because the villagers used the facilities in the city as well. Hence, our study was a wholly urban one, and we are not competent to comment on the needs of the rural masses in the state. However, the villages studied did not present a very different picture from that seen in Calcutta itself as far as mental disorder rates were concerned.

RECAPITULATION AND CONCLUSIONS

Certain ambiguities and apparent confusion have been allowed to persist regarding some aspects of the study, particularly regarding psychoses. Different types of psychoses have not been diagnosed, with the exception of some cases of depression, but demographic features of schizophrenia and affective disorders have been discussed in detail and our findings have been compared. Also, vague statements regarding difficulties in diagnosing different psychoses have been made. By way of clarification we may state that Shepherd *et al.* (1981), in their well known study, did not separate the types of psychoses either. Since general practitioners find it difficult to do so, the term 'psychoses' was used to include schizophrenia, affective disorders and organic psychosis. The point is that there cannot be any objection to using the omnibus term 'psychoses' for its sub-types. Demographic features of the sub-types can also be taken as relevant for the whole. It is possible that among our cases there is yet another type of psychosis.

Indian researchers are trying to establish a 'third variety' or an 'acute psychosis with good outcome' (Kapur and Pandurangi, 1979; Kala *et al.*, 1986). We believe that it is an 'interform', i.e., affective in its form (periodicity and temporality) but schizophrenic in content. Our broad group of psychoses includes this type in large numbers, in addition to the classical types. We have also categorised psychoses as 'disturbed' and 'quiet', which is totally unconventional. The rationale being that the urgency of hospitalisation was only applicable to the disturbed type, both from medical or objective and from social perspectives. The proportion of such cases to the total number of longstanding psychoses (33 per cent in the present study) gives us some idea of the demand for mental hospital beds. Of course, this is not to suggest that the other types do not require treatment, but they are better suited for community care. The cases diagnosed as 'depressed' were evaluated as such only with unmistakable evidence. We believed that valuable information would be lost if these cases were not recorded as such, because it showed that severe cases of depression with its life threatening propensities were rather uncommon (approximately 0.14 per cent of adults at risk). It may be asked whether similar evidence could not be obtained for chronic cases of schizophrenia. As stated earlier, we believe that the majority of longstanding cases of psychoses are undifferentiated and diagnosis is difficult even in a clinic setting.

The category termed 'abnormal personality' may appear to be most confusing; the term has been applied to cases, not on the basis of an examination of the personality dimensions, but on the basis of conduct manifestations. We may point out here that even in international classifications, there is confusion in this area. We were unable to delineate the 'personality disorders' of DSM III (APA, 1980) from the 'conduct disorders' of ICD-9 (WHO, 1978a). However, we have termed the condition 'personality disorder' (which gives it a definitive stamp without proper justification) rather than conduct disorder, because this latter term would have been more confusing as 'psychosis' in the present study was categorised mainly on the basis of conduct (and labelling). To add another dimension to it without theoretical support would have been illogical. As we have stressed the possibility of an 'arrested' form of psychosis as an aetiological background of this condition, 'query psychosis' (? psychosis) would have been its best ascription. This was however rejected because, in that case, its similarity with ICD-9 (WHO. 1978a) or DSM III (APA, 1980) categories would not have been noticed and it would have appeared solely as a result of diagnostic difficulty.

Our open minded approach has been vindicated by the observation of a psychiatric condition in large numbers, which was not detected in earlier Indian studies.

We cannot make much claim regarding psychosis, apart from the fact that a group of longstanding cases was found which could be sharply differentiated from neurotics. Within the psychotic group, there were overlaps between the sub-categories, but within the parameters there is no theoretical obfuscation.

Our approach to psychoneuroses was rather tentative to begin with, but it was vindicated by a later study by Sandel (1982) who also established the validity of the instrument used (the IRS). The test-retest reliability study was conducted later by another colleague. Though the sub-categories of neuroses were loosely made (the details have been listed with the morbidity rates), they parallel with the afore-mentioned study, the majority in both studies complained of anxiety-depressive type of symptoms. Though the large study had covered only 'fits', conversion hysteria, etc., were also observed but rather infrequently.

We did not come across any of the so-called culture bound syndromes. The specific Indian one, that is, *dhaat* or *jiriyan* could have been missed, because questions pertaining to sexual problems were avoided so as not to antagonise the respondents. The only culture influenced conditions observed were (probably) abnormal personality, possession state and *suchi-bai* (purity mania), all of these were noted in large numbers and have been discussed earlier in detail.

An overall assessment of mental health in Calcutta showed a low rate of psychoses, and a high rate of neuroses. These rates have been compared with rates obtained in other field surveys in India. It was found that our rate of psychoses (5.04/1000) was at the lower end of the range, but if 'personality disorders' were added to it (8.2/1000), then it approached the upper limit of psychoses rates in India. Psychoneuroses rate (74.8/1000) in Calcutta was much higher than that observed elsewhere in India. It was also seen that rates for retardation, epilepsy and geriatric problems were very close to estimates or observed rates in different parts of India. It must be noted that comparisons have been made with only those epidemiological studies which were conducted in urban areas and followed proper sampling procedures.

For the sake of interest, the rates obtained by a study in London (Shepherd *et al.*, 1981) may be quoted:

Psychoses	5.9/1000 at risk
Mental Subnormality	2.3/1000 at risk
Dementia	1.4/1000 at risk
Neuroses	88.5/1000 at risk
Personality Disorder	5.5/1000 at risk

For neuroses the sex differences was 55.7 for males and 116.6 for females (per 1000 at risk).

Sex difference in neuroses in our study was 68.2 for males and 161.8 for females (per 1000 of respective sexes at risk).

It may be reiterated that we do not claim that our findings are a true reflection of psychiatric disorders in Calcutta, we had only recorded what was revealed to us. However, if our findings are taken as approximations of 'true' figures then it will be seen that they are very similar to above figures, specially for the two major categories.

Shepherd *et al.* (1981) have quoted studies where prevalence rates for psychoses in different parts of the world have ranged from 3.8 (in Taiwan) to 10.9 (in Denmark). Our figure for psychoses was found to be within this range, though for Calcutta it was 'expected' to be higher. Not only are the treatment facilities poor, but all known environmental and psychological stress factors operate in Calcutta. For the majority of the population, gross and acute poverty, poor nutrition, ill-health and infection are pervasive and enmeshed with insecurity and anxiety regarding employment, housing, and the daily hazards of travelling and living in this over-crowded city. But the effects of these stresses on the prevalence of psychoses were not easily discernible. The likelihood that cases have been under-reported can be discounted, as the rates were close to other urban rates. We would, in fact, like to know why they were not higher. Also, there is no reason to suspect that psychotics were hidden when the respondents expressed neurotic complaints in such profusion. As stated earlier, the 'stigma factor' is not very strong in Calcutta, except among the very rich (where life stresses and consequent morbidity are expected to be low). Chronic cases are difficult to hide and we had taken wandering and incarcerated cases into account (see morbidity rates).

A possible reason for the reported prevalence could be as follows: The type of psychosis that affects the local populance carries a better prognosis, suggesting that stresses or whatever aetiological factors operate lead to the breakdown, but the affected recover early, which could be due to both socio-cultural and biological reasons. Lack of chronicity in Indian patients has·been found by various authors, as noted earlier. What has been said also suggests that the incidence rate (i.e., new cases) should be high, a point which could be verified by further studies.

At this point it will be pertinent to cite Murphy's (1982) views on the effect of socio-cultural influence on mental disorders. In a discussion on schizophrenia, while comparing the most vulnerable Irish with the least vulnerable Hutterite or Tongans, Murphy (1982) observed the ratio of prevalence rates only '4/1 or 5/1 which is probably as great as one is going to meet'. Though 'the degree of international variation is limited', within the limits 'social factors affect the risk and character of the disease'. In the case of affective disorders, he reported that the socio-cultural effects were more pronounced. Social factors are 'not the obvious ones like war, poverty or loss', but are more in the sphere of social expectations, attainability of goals, complicated rules for action, mutual support or competitiveness and other such subtle factors.

We understand that these views are relevant to schizophrenia and affective disorders only, which one should not misappropriate to prove a point in a discussion of undiagnosed (or undiagnosable) prevalence rates of psychoses; however, the near parity of disorder rates across cultures seems to lead to a devaluation of socio-cultural factors in the causation of psychoses, and it is in this area that Murphy's (1982) views give certain direction for further research.

As mentioned earlier, in the case of psychoneuroses, our study was strongly supported by Sandel (1982). One of the nagging doubts that persisted was related to the diagnosis of neuroses. Can we call these complainers, picked out by our locally devised instrument, 'true' cases of neurosis? This question was adequately answered by Sandel (1982), who believed that had we used a highly reputed instrument such as the 'Present State Examination' (Wing *et al.*, 1974), the result would have been the same. But Sandel reported that her clinical evaluation would have rendered about 20 per cent of the 'cases' subclinical. Another issue that was resolved by Sandel's study was that symptom patterns of the diagnosed clinic cases and those of 'field cases' were much the same; or it may be said that most of the complaints qualified as symptoms, but they differed in severity and intensity.

The prevalence rate of neuroses can be claimed to be a fair approximation, at least as judged by the psychiatrist's usual perception of neuroses. Psychoneuroses were common in Calcutta, particularly among Bengali women. The possible reasons were the usual stress factors mentioned earlier. The respondents blamed adverse circumstances for their complaints. Sandel (1982) has also shown that adverse circumstances in the form of life events and difficulties were highly significant among cases. But she also reported that these were present in large numbers among asymptomatic women as well. She concluded that some fairly effective coping mechanism was operating in the community. It is also possible that where the stresses are overwhelming, some self-protective forces operate against life-threatening psychoses.

Psychiatric disorders have been found to be more common among women all over the world; a finding which is strongly supported by our study. Besides stressful life events, which are also more common among women, changing sex roles is thought to be one of the main causal factors in the genesis of depression in women (Brown and Harris, 1978). The Bengali social milieu has undergone profound changes since the Second World War, and along with this the social roles of Bengali women have also changed significantly. However, the new roles are ill-defined and ambiguous. Bengali women are increasingly expected to shoulder a greater share of family responsibilities and remain self-reliant with little support from their husbands. It may be hypothesised that in the prevailing conditions of extreme insecurity, these expectations have produced a sense of helplessness and powerlessness in Bengali women, which has further added to the distress. We found a high level of distress where these feelings were most manifest, that is, among economically dependent women and those with little or no education. Those who lacked education probably perceived it as a key to 'power', through which the external world could be comprehended and controlled. In an attempt to explain why Bengali women are more affected than non-Bengali women, it may be said that social changes in Bengal have been more profound and have persisted for a longer time. Perhaps awareness of self and society is also stronger in Bengali women. However, it must be emphasised that the whole problem of roles is closely related to social class, which requires deep sociological analysis.

To recapitulate the main findings related to the variables, it was observed that sex and age had a clear association with psychiatric disorders—women and those in the older age groups were most vulnerable. Widows were extremely vulnerable, married men and single women were less vulnerable. Economic and occupational status were rather inconsistently related, but in certain aspects and age groups, the lower levels of the community were more affected, particularly males as far as psychoses and related disorders were concerned, and females as far as neuroses and related disorders were concerned. Low levels of education were strongly associated with the disorders. There was evidence of a higher degree of distress among the poorer sections in the suburbs and hinterlands of Calcutta, though some tentative suggestions have been made the reasons remain obscure. Women in low level occupations and in certain social roles were more affected, especially economically dependent elderly women. Members of joint families were better protected than those of nuclear families, but transitional families were the most vulnerable.

It will be seen that the findings regarding these correlates more or less agree with the broad trends in demography and ecology accepted as high risk by different studies all over the world.

The World Health Organisation (1975) concluded some years ago that 'well conducted epidemiological studies in several parts of the world have shown no fundamental differences either in the range of mental disorders that occur or in the prevalence of seriously incapacitating mental illness.' Though we fully endorse this statement, yet it leaves a puzzling question unanswered. It has been said that mental disorders with an organic basis (such as, nutritional, infective and traumatic) occur more frequently in the developing countries (WHO, 1975; Giel, 1975). Though we could not detect these types of disorders in spite of the health examination of the sampled population, we do not claim that they were absent. The question why the rates were not influenced by this factor, can be reformulated by asking whether these could have been even lower if the organic factor was not present.

In addition, the present study established:

1. The extent of minor psychiatric disorders. Doubts have been expressed that these may 'remain undetected under various guises' in developing countries (WHO, 1975). Our findings suggest that many of the assumptions regarding hidden illness are doubtful, particularly the theories of somatisation. We found that somatisers were not using 'guises' for their psychological distress. They would freely complain provided they were given an opportunity. Neurosis is a matter of social evaluation and medical perception.

2. For an urban population in a developing country, demographic correlates of mental disorders in the community were shown to be almost similar to those found in major studies in other parts of the world.

One of the important aims of this study was to find evidence of the effects of poverty and urban stresses on the people of Calcutta. It was observed that 20 per cent of the population was living under abject poverty, another 60 per cent was above the so-called poverty line, but still poor by all standards. The remaining 20 per cent was somewhat affluent, but real affluence was seen only in 5 per cent. It is said (Leighton, 1959) that poverty gives rise to social disintegration, which results in parental quarrels, broken marriages, neglect of children and a weak network of communication. The breadwinner tends to desert, leading to role reversal (that is, the mother takes on the father's role which confuses the children). However, we found little evidence of this. Fatherless families we encountered were ones where the father had died. It is also said that the culture of poverty (Finney, 1970) is basically a psychological problem, 'a feeling of not belonging . . . the institutions of the larger society are not there for their interest . . . it is a feeling of alienation, of cynicism, of purposelessness, of rootlessness, of anomie.' Finney (1970) also observed that 'the poor in India do not live in a culture of poverty, basic religious concept binds him to the whole.' As far as the poor in Calcutta are concerned, we endorse this view, we also agree that basic social cohesion and the remarkably resilient family system were the results of a 'binding religious concept.' We had enquired into religious beliefs and found that only about 4 per cent of the families did not perform some daily religious ritual or maintain pollution rules. There was no religion, community or class where one or the other or both were not observed. The insignificance of the number of families transgressing these fundamental practices indicates that religion is still an active force among Indian urbanites. However, we are not offering any apology for poverty or claiming that the degradation and misery of poverty were not felt by the Indian poor. People believed that a large part of their unhappiness and neurotic complaints were due to poverty.

A potent source of social disruption and mental disorders is believed to be migration, urbanisation and rapid social change (Clifford, 1966; Plog, 1969). As discussed earlier, Calcutta has borne the brunt of one of the most massive migrations in history, when the nation was partitioned. In addition, rural to urban migration has been continuing for decades. It was a common, rather pedestrian expectation that these factors would lead to disruption and disorganisation of the community, but at the same time it was noticed that the effects on mental disorder rates (or even crime) were not very great (Chakraborty,

1978). The present study reported that the areas surrounding Calcutta had greater distress and, consequently, higher rates. It has been argued that the causes were not the usual types of migration, but it was probably due to the settlement of refugees from the eastern parts of Bengal (which is now the sovereign state of Bangladesh). We agree with Macpherson (1983) that urbanisation *per se* does not give rise to much disorganisation, and the mental health of migrants need not necessarily be poor. It would seem that rural to urban migration from the nearby rural areas to the outskirts of Calcutta, followed a certain pattern—slow and gradual assimilation, communication and active contact with the villages of origin and close network of support. There was not much evidence of any painful change in the life-style of the new migrants or high rates of mental disorders. Of course, it goes without saying that they were most distressed by gross poverty. Migrations are of different types and the effects vary, the consequential urbanisation cannot be blamed for all psychological ills in developing countries.

The primary aim of the present study was to determine the volume and extent of mental disorders in Calcutta in order to help planners in instituting remedial measures. Though the aim was fulfilled as far as we are concerned, it is doubtful whether planners will ever take any notice of it, though the survey was initiated by the largest planning body of the country. Such is the fate of most surveys (Higginbotham, 1979). However, we are fortunate to have a National Mental Health Programme (initiated through the laudable efforts of Professor N.N. Wig, 1982). On account of such plans, the practical value of the study may have been somewhat negated, but it is our modest claim that this study, being one of the largest urban mental health studies to date, will throw some light on the basic and fundamental problems of psychiatry that are particularly relevant in the Indian context.

ILLUSTRATIVE HISTORIES

Random Cases

Uneducated widow (39), working as a maid servant, has four children. The eldest daughter (19) had some schooling and worked in a factory. She was found to be irritable, asocial and suspicious. Her son, aged 17, was also irritable and suspicious. He had no schooling because he was dull and was unemployed. Another daughter, 15 years old, was neither studying nor working. She had no complaints. The youngest son (14 years) was said to be very naughty. He was always fighting and playing truant.

The respondent's husband died at the age of 35. His sister who was well educated and worked in an office, helped the family after his death. They were middle class before they were beset by financial problems. A real 'problem family' with acute financial and mental health problems. The children were dull and very irritable. They had become delinquents. The mother was physically ill and acutely anxious. (The eldest son slapped the mother to stop her from talking to the investigators).

Female teacher (36), living with a female relative (20). Both unmarried and of high status. She answered all the questions in the negative, and was irritated by those on depression. She said that what was the use of answering these questions and burst into tears. The relative had tuberculosis, but had undergone treatment and had recovered. She seemed unmindful of the fact of not being able to study. She complained of somatic and sleep problems, as well as of several anxiety symptoms.

Widow (43) has three sons, the eldest was 19. She complained of weakness, and said that she thought so much of family problems that she did not feel like working, and her son's earning was not enough to buy food for four people. Her sons were always falling sick, and she felt so unhappy and helpless that she did not feel like doing any work. Her mind would become sad for no reason.

Widow (37) has five children. The eldest daughter's husband looked after all of them. She complained of feeling helpless.

Widow (35), well-off, owned a house, has four sons and one daughter. Her elder brother who lived with the family and acted as the 'head', recently got married and moved out. Since then, she has felt very helpless and depressed. One son (aged 19) was anti-social, addict, irritable, dull and had delayed development. Another son (aged 17) was depressed about family affairs and his brother. He said that he did not feel like studying or working. Another son (aged 15), had polio, and was crippled.

Widow (42) has two sons and two daughters. All children were studying. The family lived on a small Railway pension. No one had any complaints. The eldest daughter suffered from *suchi-bai*.

Single woman (48), clerk, lived with two younger brothers aged 24 and 20 years. Though both had college education, yet they were unemployed. No one had any complaints. She suffered from heart disease.

Widow (30), maid servant, her husband had leprosy. Her son (aged 12) also developed it at the age of 4. The disease was quiescent. She suffered from 'fits', and her employer was getting her treated. According to the doctors, fits were due to anaemia. She also complained of insomnia and anxiety symptoms.

Widow (50) has two sons and two daughters. The eldest daughter worked in a factory and supported the family. The eldest son was mentally ill. He had been attending the OPD for treatment. Though he was quiet, he was neither working nor studying. The daughter was worried about her responsibility, and as a result had somatic and sleep problems. The mother was severely depressed, she was bedridden with sciatica a few weeks ago.

Two widows (aged 55 and 60 years) 'co-wives'. The younger one did a little tailoring. Her only son suddenly died 10 years ago, since then she has had multiple complaints.

The family of a widow, son, son's wife and their three children. Almost destitute. The children had malnutrition. The son was a bus conductor, but he drank and smoked *ganja*, beat his wife and mother, and got into trouble with the police almost daily. The mother had severe obsessional and various other symptoms. The son's wife was a timid person and was very scared of her husband. She was suffering from 'fits' after the last child was born (epilepsy), she also had several anxiety symptoms.

Widow (55), owned a house and property, she insisted that as her sons were not at home, the investigators should be brief. In the course of the conversation, a shadow appeared on a glass partition, and a loud male voice started talking. He answered questions, but refused to come out. The woman took the investigator outside the house and gave the history of her son's illness, who had been so for the last 10 years. Medical as well as healer's treatment had failed. He was extremely irritable, and remained in his room throughout the day and night and talked to himself. Her other sons lived nearby and quarrelled over the property. She herself was 'going mad' with worries, she also had many anxiety symptoms. (The Investigator showed considerable tact and competence in obtaining the information. The interview with the shadow, of course, had to be declared 'unreliable'.)

Widow (60), *ayah* in a private nursing home. Since husband's death several years ago, she has faced acute financial problems. Of her five children, only one was working. Two younger daughters had left studies to look after the household. One of them had epilepsy (treated by doctors). The head (mother) had always been nervous, and suffered from depression, and was irritable.

Housewife (60), her daughter (29) and her husband lived together. The husband was in hospital. One son (aged 18) had fallen from a tree and had died. She admitted that she was given to washing and cleaning 'always'. Since her son's death, worries made her 'feel choked', she said that what was the use of living, that she should seek treatment. Her daughter, a maid servant, 'always' washed and cleaned, and could not stand the sight of knives. She had no sleep since her brother died. The mother also had sleep problems, anxiety and depression.

Retired man (75), owned a house. He had tuberculosis which was active again. He also suffered from asthma. Two sons lived with him. He lived with his daughter in the ground floor flat as he had disagreement with his sons. He manifested anxiety symptoms which were due to physical problems.

Widow (40) belonging to the lowest strata. Her husband died 3 months ago, and her son-in-law was supporting her. She complained of problems relating to sleep, anxiety, as well as obsessional and phobic symptoms.

Unemployed man (22), his mother was a maid servant. Belonged to the lowest strata. For one year he had sleep problems, anxiety, depression. He said that he thought about finding a job all the time and as a result he could not sleep or eat.

Two sisters, both over 60 years, living together. Manage through 'help' (source obscure). The elder one had become 'mad', since her husband's death. She refused to talk or interact, was suspicious, would laugh, cry, mutter throughout the day. The younger sister complained of somatic problems, sleep, anxiety, and depression. She said, 'I have nobody, how long can I go on, who will look after [my] mad sister when I die?'

Mother and daughter, both widows, aged 75 years and 60 years respectively. Belonged to the agriculturist caste. The daughter made paper bags and was in the habit of drinking. Neither of them had any complaints. (The daughter's son lived separately with his family, and did not help his mother and grandmother). Comment—it is very unusual for a Bengali Hindu female to drink.

Woman (24), gave her occupation as prostitution. She lived with a man who was a good football player. She left home, as her husband married a second time. She felt her profession did not 'suit' her, as her health was running down. All the symptoms had started after she left home. She answered all questions including feeling of suffocation in a closed room in the affirmative (pan-neurosis).

Muslim boy (21), a worker. Widowed mother, a younger brother (who had tuberculosis), and an unmarried sister lived together. He felt very restless at times, but did not know why. He complained of a jammed head, weakness, and had no sleep for the last 2–3 years.

Widow (55), has seven sons and one daughter. Only the eldest son was working as a watchman on a very small salary. All children had high school education. Nobody had any complaints.

Married woman (60), husband (65), one daughter (25) was working, two sons were unemployed, all including the husband were educated. The mother was illiterate, and was described as dull and looked it. She was always jolly, laughed excessively, could not understand anything complicated, but managed the household and cooking. Dullness was believed to be caused by typhoid which she had at 10 years of age. She was married off by the time she was 11 years old.

Retired man (68), Christian, well-to-do, was an insurance agent, had high blood pressure, would forget and make mistakes, was severely obsessional. His son, a graduate, was unemployed, as a result 'constant thoughts going round my head, don't feel like doing any work.'

Married woman (30), her husband (45) was a labourer. She had two caesarians and said, 'my husband is getting old. I sometimes go mad with worries.' Complained of weakness after the caesarian operation and suffered from many anxiety symptoms.

---

v (15) of middle strata neither studying nor working, widowed mother worked in a factory, had three younger brothers. He complained of anxiety and depressive symptoms, but refused to elaborate.

Girl (16) of middle economic strata and education. She said, 'I used to get "fits" when I was young because of worms (doctors said); now I get it only when I am sad. I get very sad for mother (dead) and brother' (nothing wrong with him). On being asked why, she started crying (no further questioning, in case she had fits). She had got married recently, and had come to her father's for a visit, fits were less since marriage. The eldest of five siblings. The father was a peon. Her younger sister was mildly retarded (began walking at the age of 4), she was attending school, but was in a class lower than her age group).

A North Calcutta Neighbourhood

A middle status Brahmin family. The father (65) was a priest, the mother (55) a maid servant, one son (25) was a tea vendor (married with two children), and another son (20) worked as a helper to a goldsmith. No one apart from the father had more than elementary education. The younger son was depressed, and felt helpless and useless as he could not get a job. He had got married recently. (Comment—the sons had not followed their father's profession, dire poverty had reduced their social status, as indicated by their lack of schooling and low status occupations. One uncle was a military officer).

Labourer (40), wife (35), three daughters aged 18, 13 and 8 years. He was not available at home on three occasions, but 2 months later he was suffering from ascites, and complained of severe anxiety.

Head (63) owned a small electric repair shop. Had three sons and two daughters. Wife (45) complained of severe burning sensations and lack of sleep since she had ligation operation. The eldest son was B.Com., but was unemployed. The other two sons had little education and helped in the shop. The father was worried as the boys were disobedient. The eldest son complained of several depressive symptoms.

A family of ten members, all with college education and high status occupations. There was a case of suicide in the family; but no one had any complaints.

Young man (18), father (45) was a clerk, mother (38) was a housewife. Only son whose development was delayed, but he was not dull. He refused to study or work, and wandered about the whole day. He suffered from violent temper outbursts. The father wanted to know whether there was any treatment for this, as he may even commit a murder.

Young man (aged 24), Railway worker. He said that his wife was extremely suspicious about his character. She fought so much that he would wander around after work and dared not return home. While wandering, he would 'imagine' his wife's allegations as real, which made him laugh and (sometimes) even mutter. On questioning, the wife would not elaborate, but complained of having 'fits'. The man was in 'Mao-tse-Tung's party' for some years. (A neighbour informed that the couple had the most violent fights and that they 'both were mad').

Head (55), illiterate, sign painter; wife (40), hospital *ayah*: five children. Status—low. The eldest son was an active party worker and had been convicted for two and a half years during the emergency. He claimed that he was severely beaten up and 'even now getting pains in the head'. He finds being unemployed unbearable, worries all the time and cannot sleep.

Well-to-do man (46), property owner, did not talk to anybody, was annoyed if any member of the family was found talking. He suffered from occasional violent outbursts of temper. His wife (41) complained of many neurotic symptoms which had persisted for many years, she could not sleep. A nephew (23) who lived with them, did not work, and wandered around, 'always getting into fights.'

Housewife (33), severe case of *suchi-bai*. She said that it was mild earlier and had become much worse after refusing a beggar, but 'really because of weakness and bad health.' Her husband (36) was a proof-reader, but was 'not well' for last few months, making mistakes and checking everything repeatedly.

A Family Story

Fourteen members in this middle class family. Father (65) had a history of mental illness, he was treated and was quite well (did not elaborate), and was working as a clerk. Mother was mentally ill, was under treatment from a doctor, but appeared to be quite well. For ten years she had complained of severe burning of the body and head. She would tear her hair and would scratch herself till she bled, she would run out of the house and behave 'as if mad'. (Treatment suggested—psychotic depression). Her son (33), a clerk, said that he had no sleep all night, because of worrying too much as he was also suffering from 'burning sensations like mother', especially during full moon. He was an active leftist political worker, who 'taught their village doctor a lesson' for pilfering drugs, by making the doctor's wife dress in a widow's clothes. But now a curse was on him! First, his wife died, then his daughter fell into an oven and died. He was losing weight as his 'blood had turned bad' (requested a blood examination). Daughter (37) became a widow and shifted to her father's house along with her three children. She was suffering from some skin disease on her left arm, which was not responding to any treatment. She complained of headache, giddiness, weakness, insomnia and excessive worries related to her children's future. Another daughter (aged 25), would be beaten up by her husband who finally left her at her father's house with one sick boy (keeping the other two children himself). She complained that her body burned, she felt weak, sad and helpless. Loss of interest and excessive cleanliness were recent developments. ...t fears (phobic type) were present since childhood.

Addendum

An In-depth Study of Neurosis Among Women in Calcutta (With Special Reference to Life Events)

DR. B. SANDEL

MBBS, DPM, MD (Psych), MRC (Psych)

WHAT IS NEUROSIS

THE term neurosis, coined in 1769 by William Cullen, originally denoted a 'generalised affection of the nervous system' that did not seem to be caused by either localised disease or febrile illness. Today, it has come to acquire four different meanings. First, in a non-technical sense, it refers to someone who over-reacts to relatively trivial life events with anxiety, depression or other such complaint. Second, the medical or psychiatric use referring to the neurotic syndromes. Third, the word 'neuroticism' as used by psychologists as a measure of how neurotic people are, though this is not identical with the medical concept. Fourth, as in 'neurotic' character disorder, in which the disorder lies in the way in which a person forms relationships with others, there often being no symptoms in the ordinary sense of the word.

Consideration of the use of the term in psychiatry is essential since it continues to survive, appearing in new British textbooks of psychiatry (Gelder *et al.*, 1983; Russell and Hersov, 1983) despite the recent serious attempt to abandon it (Spitzer *et al.*, 1980). We will consider the arguments for and against the concept by examining the traditionally accepted defining characteristics stated in the International Classification of Diseases—9th revision (WHO, 1978)

> Neurotic disorders are mental disorders without any demonstrable organic basis in which the patient may have considerable insight and has unimpaired reality testing, in that he does not confuse his morbid subjective experiences and fantasies with external reality. Behaviour may be greatly affected although usually remaining within socially acceptable limits, but personality is not disorganized.

While neurotic syndromes may frequently appear in persons with organic disease of various parts of the body (Lishman, 1978), these are commonly viewed as reactions to the physical condition rather than as being intrinsically caused by it. Conditions such as apoplexy and epilepsy, which were listed under neuroses in Cullen's time, are now classified elsewhere, following a clearer understanding of the pathological processes involved, as have others more recently discerned to be organic rather than hysterical, viz., spasmodic torticollis, globus hystericus and writer's cramp. Another aetiological assumption that has engendered much controversy originated in the work of psychoanalytic thinkers, extending the meaning of the term neurosis to include the psychopathological process through which the conditions were supposed to arise. Debate surrounding these issues has culminated in major changes in the third edition of the Diagnostic and Statistical Manual of Mental Disorders (APA, 1980) and will be discussed in further detail.

Nowhere has the disagreement over the several dichotomous systems of psychiatric classification been more complex than in the case of depression, namely, the issue of endogenous versus reactive, and psychotic versus neurotic depression. The view of neurosis as implying a reaction to stress, though differing from the natural response of normal individuals to stress in being exaggerated and out of proportion to the stress, is no longer valid, as research has shown stress to be important in most categories of mental disorders, life events and constitutional factors contributing to both 'reactive' and the so-called endogenous syndromes (Kendell and Zealley, 1983). The presence of morbid subjective experiences such as hallucinations and delusions, loss of insight and impaired reality testing remain more descriptive of psychotic phenomena though several issues related to the detection of insight in clinical practice remain unresolved. When these symptoms are manifested, a diagnosis of neurosis is highly unlikely, though not impossible, as hallucinations may occur in bereavement reactions and poor insight may accompany obsessive-compulsive disorder.

Snaith (1980) and others have asserted that psychoses and neuroses do not form distinct, mutually exclusive categories, and have suggested that neuroses lie on a continuum of abnormality, between normality on the one hand and psychoses on the other. Others have proposed a class of borderline conditions in which neurotic and psychotic mechanisms occur simultaneously (Noyes, 1955), or, which are inter-mediate between schizophrenia and neuroses, and neuroses and personality disorder (Gelder, 1986). An interesting though little used approach to these issues is contained in Foulds' hierarchical model of personal illness (1976), which accommodates the common observation of psychiatric symptoms in normals, and the presence of symptoms from the 'lower' categories of illness (such as neuroses) in patients diagnosable as suffering from disorders in a 'higher' category (such as organic psychiatric syndromes). A similar hierarchy operates in clinical practice where priority is given to certain diagnoses despite concurrent symptoms of less serious disorders.

These debates on what constitutes neuroses are reflected in the major systems of classification, and changes in the trends in psychiatry following the influence of psychoanalysis and the social sciences on medicine are revealed in subsequent modifications of these systems. Mayer-Gross and associates' textbook (1954) lists a number of 'Special Forms of Reaction and of Personality', viz., depressive, neurasthenic, anxiety and phobic, hysterical, and paranoid reactions, along with obsessional states, anorexia nervosa, irritability, hypochondriasis, depersonalization and three personality types. The ICD–9 (WHO, 1978) no longer emphasises the reactive nature of these conditions and substitutes instead an immensely broad range of 'neurotic disorders' which can be distinguished in terms of their non-psychotic and non-organic character. In other words, it shifts from an aetiological underpinning for classification to a mixed descriptive and aetiological one, and retains most of the sub-types mentioned earlier. The American Psychiatric Association's Diagnostic and Statistical Manual–II (1968) incorporated a similar viewpoint although relying more on psychoanalytically derived inferences.

The DSM III (APA, 1980) as mentioned earlier, has abandoned the category of neuroses altogether, prompted by a theoretical dispute in American psychiatry over the psychodynamics and criticisms of low scientific testability and reliability of such concepts. Spitzer *et al.* (1977) have argued that intrapsychic conflict is seen in so many psychiatric disorders as well as in persons who do not suffer from any psychiatric disorder, that the traditional category of neuroses, with its psychoanalytic implication of an aetiology based on conflict resolution by the process of symptom formation, has little to recommend it. The new system therefore reallocates the sub-types of neurotic illness to various other categories of disease classification on the basis of behavioural and overt symptoms. It also adopts a multi-axial system to include the additional information on premorbid personality and psychosocial stressors, as well as the coexistence of other non-psychiatric disorders. Other significant changes involve the grouping of depressive neurosis, renamed dysthymic disorder, with affective disorders, and the inclusion of obsessive-compulsive disorders under anxiety disorder. More radical differences arise in the treatment of the old category of hysteria, which is substituted by the creation of three new categories, namely, somatoform disorders, dissociative disorders and factitious disorders. While the inclusion of depersonalisation disorder with the dissociative disorders, with which it has very little in common, offers doubtful benefits, the new class of factitious disorders, in which uncommon self-inflicted disorders can be included, is potentially useful. Another addition which has led to some debate regarding its validity as an entity, is somatisation disorder also known as Briquet's syndrome or St. Louis Hysteria (Chodoff, 1974). Protagonists of the syndrome emphasise its organic-somatic and genetic components and avoid the psychological or psychiatric explanations while others view it as a particular pattern of abnormal illness behaviour within middle class American psychiatric practice (Thorley, 1986).

This proliferation of subcategories of hysteria in DSM III further highlights the problem of reliability of psychiatric diagnoses, despite the assertion of the APA task force responsible for the revisions, as well as the validity of some of the newer categories. While the reliability for neuroses is substantially lower than that for organic psychiatric and psychotic illness, that for the subtypes of neuroses is even poorer (Kreitman, 1961). The introduction of operational definitions of symptoms, as in the Present State Examination (Wing *et al.*, 1974), and of syndromes, as in the DSM III, are an effort to overcome this, but increased reliability of measurement cannot be taken to be a reflection of the validity of a syndrome.

The Population at Risk

Along with the refining of psychiatric nomenclature and classification, research has proliferated in the areas of epidemiology and socio-cultural antecedents of the disorders. As implied earlier, concepts of disease are inextricably linked to the concepts of predisposition, whether due to organic or developmental factors, and to those of precipitation, whether as a result of environmental stressors or biological threats.

Demographic data derived from hospital and community surveys of neurotic patients help to generate ideas regarding the population at risk of developing a disorder, which stimulate further research for the clarification of causality. Srole *et al.* (1962) defined a demographic factor as a '. . . culturally significant property or condition, differentially manifested by all individuals, that provides a basis for classifying a population into a limited series of social segments or groups.' These include 'independent' factors, such as age, sex and ethnic type, and 'interdependent' or reciprocal factors, such as marital and socio-economic status, which may vary with the subject's actions and therefore with his physical and mental health. A true picture of the distribution and symptom characteristics of a condition necessitates community studies, so that variables such as the availability of hospital based statistics may be avoided. In addition to these factors which produce bias, in-patient or even out-patient populations represent the more severe forms of the illness, particularly in countries where medical resources are scarce and expensive and treatment is directed towards those causing most disruption to society.

AN IN-DEPTH STUDY OF MINOR PSYCHIATRIC DISORDER

Aims and Methods

A study conducted in Calcutta in 1982–83 examined neuroses in depth, as they appeared in the context of urban Bengali culture. It was decided that as the manifestations of the disorder were likely to be varied in different settings the study would focus on two samples: (a) a sample of patients diagnosed and under treatment for neurotic disorders at psychiatric outpatient clinics; and (b) a sample of women in the community, where we expected to find some with neurotic symptoms.

Neurotic symptom patterns in the two groups were to be compared. The second group, we believed, would include women who were between the two extremes of normality and clinically severe pathology., as well as the intervening range of persons manifesting symptoms yet not amounting to 'cases' of neurosis. The community sample was so selected that there were approximately equal numbers from the four social classes which was expected to reflect a wide range of life circumstances and life experiences essential for the second aim of the study, i.e., to explore the nature and meaning of stress in urban Bengali culture, with particular reference to the lives of women. Further, an attempt was also made to determine the causal links, if any, between stress and neurosis.

A subsidiary aim of the study was to assess the validity of the Individual Report Schedule (Chakraborty, 1978b) as a screening instrument for the detection of neurosis in the community. This instrument was devised for a large community mental health survey (CMDA Report, 1983) and administered by trained non-medical interviewers; we wanted to compare the scores between the two samples of women so as to evaluate its efficacy in distinguishing between symptomatic normals and illness of clinical severity.

The study was conducted at the psychiatric clinic of the Institute of Postgraduate Medical Education and Research in Calcutta. As neurosis appears to affect women in far larger numbers, we focused on adult women between 14 and 60 years of age, excluding all those with mental handicap, psychosis and organic psychiatric syndromes. The following method was adopted. Two women diagnosed by the consultant psychiatrist at the outpatient clinic as suffering from neurotic disorder were examined by the author on each clinic day until a total of 30 cases had been seen. The relative accompanying each patient to the clinic was also interviewed for detailed and corroborative information, particularly regarding life stresses.

For the community sample, it was decided to interview approximately 200 women, which would yield 30 'cases' for comparison with the OPD sample. A community case rate of 15 per cent of psychoneurosis among women of Calcutta was gleaned from the CMDA Health Survey. For the community study, we selected a number of neighbourhoods in Calcutta which had a relatively homogeneous composition in terms of social class. Often a key person was known to us, in other areas such a key person was identified and contacted. Individual households were visited and after explaining the purpose of the study, women between 14 and 60 years of age were interviewed by the author. Again, cases of mental handicap, psychosis or organic psychiatric illness were excluded, as were all those who expressed a reluctance to participate in the study. Since the information we intended to obtain was of an intimately personal nature, great care was taken to establish rapport and to assess the degree of veracity and accuracy of the reports. A sample of 180 women were interviewed in this way. Special mention needs to be made of the method adopted to ascertain the social class of the respondents. The locality of residence (or *para* in Bengali) is a good indicator of social class in Calcutta, and residents of each area were questioned about their estimation of their own social position and that of their neighbours. This also helped to identify families of different classes in neighbourhoods which were not homogeneous in composition. It was found that such 'subjective' ratings by the respondents themselves were better indicators of the nuances of social class than occupation of the 'head' of the household, and it has been reported in other studies that such measures correlate well with other social indices (Brown and Harris, 1978). Furthermore, an assessment of economic level through enquiries about a family's material assets would have been difficult as such enquiries frequently aroused suspicion and hostility.

An advantage of conducting these interviews in the subjects' homes was that it was possible to observe the life styles and conditions of living directly as well as the codes of social behaviour that differentiated between the subcultures of each class. For example, private interviews with subjects were particularly difficult in most working class homes where space was limited but families were large. In traditional upper class homes on the other hand, the difficulties arose for quite different reasons with younger women (daughters or daughters-in-law) being chaperoned by an older female member of the family.

INSTRUMENTS

Each subject was interviewed using the following:

1. The Demography Schedule.
2. The Individual Report Schedule (IR Schedule). Only those who scored above 2 points on this instrument were then administered the Present State Examination.
3. The Present State Examination of Wing, Cooper and Sartorious (1974 shortened neurotic version—Bengali translation).
4. All subjects were administered the Life Events and Difficulties Schedule.

THE DEMOGRAPHY SCHEDULE

Data were obtained regarding family structure and size, individual demographic characteristics and the position of the subject in the family system. Personal details including personality types, menstrual and obstetric history, and past history of physical and mental illness were also recorded.

THE INDIVIDUAL REPORT SCHEDULE (CHAKRABORTY, 1978b)

This short interviewer rated instrument was designed for the afore-mentioned community health survey, it incorporates the most common and most important symptoms of neurotic illness. Each item rated 'present' scored 1 point. However, if it was present since childhood, the item was then rated not as a 'symptom', but as indicating a 'personality' factor.

Detailed enquiries were made regarding bodily symptoms, and only if they could not be explained on any organic basis and were severely distressing or of long duration, a score was assigned—the 'Somatisation Score'.

Sleep disturbances and the occurrence of hysterical fits were also recorded—details of the 'fit' were thoroughly examined before the possibility of true epileptic convulsions was discarded.

Before a neurotic symptom was rated as present, the respondent was asked to describe it in her own words, particularly any factors that were known to precipitate the symptom. This was important to exclude normal responses to real threats in the environment, such as brief episodes of severe anxiety in direct temporal relation to bomb explosions, as they were common phenomena in certain areas of Calcutta at that time. Each individual obtained a summed score for neurotic symptoms, personality factors and 'somatisation'. Anyone with two neurotic symptoms was then interviewed using the PSE.

THE PRESENT STATE EXAMINATION (WING *et al.*, 1974)

This is a semi-structured interview originally designed for use with hospital patients, but with subsequent extensive use in surveys of mental illness in many parts of the world, and in both patient and non-patient populations. The full version includes 140 items, and there are shorter versions for community studies or for studies of non-psychotic syndromes. Each item is rated on a 3 or 4 point scale and a detailed manual gives definitions of the symptoms to be rated and indicates the levels of symptomatology required for each point on the scale. The PSE does not include items for the diagnosis of some categories of mental disorder, i.e., alcoholism, organic states, mental retardation and personality disorder. Information regarding symptoms is collected a month before the interview, and a diagnosis arrived at according to the ICD 9 categories, if the interviewer is satisfied that there is sufficient information for a diagnosis. In nearly 25 per cent of the cases information about previous episodes and aetiology is required before a diagnosis can be made (Kendell and Zealley, 1983). The rules for making a diagnosis have been incorporated into a computer pro-gramme (CATEGO) and diagnosis is stated as one of the CATEGO classes.

Used in the prescribed manner, following a course of training, the PSE is reported to be a reliable instrument, particularly for schizo-phrenia and depressive symptoms, though the items covering anxiety are less reliable. The behavioural items are also stated to have poor inter-rater reliability.

The PSE has been used in large community studies of psychosis including the multicentric International Pilot Study of Schizophrenia (WHO, 1973) and several major studies of affective disorder.

It has also been translated into different languages and used in non-western cultures.

For the purposes of this study the shortened neurotic version of the PSE was translated into Bengali by the author. The Hindi version, translated by Professor N.N. Wig, was consulted and the Bengali translation approximated this version as far as possible while adjustments were made to suit the requirements of an urban Bengali sample. This Bengali version of the PSE was administered to psychiatric outpatients, both male and female, and where terms or expression were not comprehensible, alternative forms were used, frequently adopting the language that patients use spontaneously to express psychological distress. This was particularly important in cases where direct colloquial equivalents were not available for certain English expressions. For example, literal translations of 'difficulty in relaxing' or muscular tension (item 7) were quite incomprehensible to all persons questioned. However, they understood and often complained of 'feeling uneasy' in a physical sense, or of 'not feeling rested', when this sensation of unease was related to the limbs or neck and shoulder regions, the subject was rated as suffering from 'muscular tension', but there was confusion in differentiating between this state malaise, and bodyache or even restlessness. The last is often described in similar terms by patients, and detailed questioning was often necessary before these items could be rated.

In this study, subjects were rated for present mental state as well as for past episodes of psychological symptoms using the PSE and the Syndrome Check List (designed for this purpose). A number of patients had reported a single episode of long duration. Diagnostically important information about an earlier phase of the disorder was recorded separately. Diagnoses were then arrived at by using the CATEGO programme.

The Life Events and Difficulties Schedule

Several life events questionnaires were considered, but none were found to be suitable as large sections would have required radical changes, if they were not to be dropped altogether, in order to be acceptable to Indian subjects.

The most obvious cultural ban is on explicit discussions with persons outside the family of matters relating to sexual relationships, and this area often needs to be approached in an indirect manner. While sexual problems within a marriage may be discussed, pre-marital and extra-marital relationships are very rarely mentioned, especially keeping in view the stresses on the individual as a result of such liaisons. Questions regarding financial problems also need to be broached very gently, as mentioned earlier, and care should be exercised in the judgement of what constitutes 'stress' in a population with wide disparities in income. In both marital/sexual and economic matters, the different social classes respond very differently, and it was observed that members of the lowest class were far less reticent, while the middle and upper classes were more likely to respond to such questions with suspicion and hostility. The relationship between the reluctance to disclose intimate details of family interaction and culturally influenced 'denial' of conflict, or culturally valued notions of family harmony in non-western cultures (Kirmayer, 1984) will be examined later.

A widely researched factor in the interpersonal relationships of persons with affective disorder is the presence of social support networks and the existence of a close, confiding relationship, particularly in studies of women (Brown and Harris, 1978). Our subjects also reported such confiding relationships usually with other women, who were often family members, but very few described such a relationship with their husband. Those who did so were largely from the upper, westernised section of society, where social roles and family expectations were quite different as compared to the more traditional families, even in the same social class.

A schedule was therefore designed for this study which covered ten areas of experience including personal health, bereavements/separations as well as enquiries about stresses relating to children and the family, which was considered particularly relevant to the population under study. Emphasis was placed on certain features which were expected to affect women in particular—family; employment outside the home with reference to prejudice or discrimination against working women, and the extent of conflict between traditional mores and modern roles; interpersonal relations within the family with special attention to the delegation of authority and responsibility; conflicts between traditional and modern attitudes to marriage, dowry and inter-caste unions; conflicts pertaining to child-rearing and motherhood. Old case records of patients at the psychiatric unit were examined to delineate the kind of stresses reported spontaneously in relation to their illnesses, and records of the community mental health survey of Greater Calcutta (CMDA Report, 1983) were also examined to obtain similar information given by persons who had not consulted a psychiatrist. A list of items was drawn up in each of the ten areas, and each respondent was questioned about incidents or longer lasting problems within the year preceding the interview in the case of those who did not have any psychological symptoms, or within the year preceding the onset in case of those who had such symptoms. Incidents that occurred after the onset of illness were not recorded.

THE RATING OF LIFE EVENTS AND DIFFICULTIES

The life event methodology of Brown and Harris (1978) was adopted, with some modifications. The advantages of using this approach were twofold. First, the careful differentiation between the characteristics of the event and the individual's reaction to it. Second, the rating of 'contextual threat' of an event by attempting to measure the precise meaning which each event or difficulty would have for the average individual in the *same circumstances*. In addition to this approach, ratings for both 'event' and 'difficulty' were made under special circumstances where it was felt that an event had resulted in a set of difficult circumstances that lasted for a prolonged period causing problems quite distinct from those due to the event alone. For example, the death of a husband is a bereavement event, but in the case of an individual belonging to the lower social class, whose resources in the form of alternative source of financial support, or possibility of employment, are often severely limited, the financial stress will often warrant an additional rating as a 'difficulty'. A *life event* was defined as any incident that occurred within the specified period, involving the respondent or her family in the ten areas of the life events and difficulty schedule. The family included all persons with whom the subject lived at the time of interview, or with whom she had close emotional ties because of having lived with them for a length of time in the past. Thus, second degree relatives were often included in families which were joint in the past, but were no longer so at the time of the interview. A *difficulty* was defined as an ongoing problem that had continued for a minimum of 4 weeks within the period specified, and involved the respondent or her family in the ten specified areas. The importance of studying stresses of this nature was highlighted during the Community Mental Health Survey (CMDA, 1983) when it was found that women, especially housewives, frequently appeared to be under tremendous long term pressures despite the lack of discrete incidents or easily identifiable problems to which this distress could be related.

The enquiry also revealed the underlying causes which were often not recognised as such, since large sections of the community suffered in a similar manner, and therefore the respondents did not consider them important enough to be mentioned. For example, cramped living quarters, a constant feeling of apprehension in certain areas of the city known for lawlessness, the pervading sense of instability caused by employment on a daily basis, or anxiety relating to un-employment of son or husband, the acute physical discomfort of the public transport system for persons who were obliged to travel long distances to work. Problems such as these cut across class and income groups, though poorer sections of the population had fewer resources for coping with these problems.

Difficulties were recorded if they were experienced at the time of interview, and if they were no longer experienced, corroboration was sought from other family members to minimise errors due to altera-tions in the respondents' mental state, or due to faulty memory.

Life events and difficulties were rated according to the area of life in which maximum distress was produced, the severity of the threat and the duration of effect. When an event could be rated under more than one heading, the one selected was dictated by the severity of effect. For example, an induced abortion in a 35 year old middle class mother of two teenaged children was rated as socio-sexual rather than under health, since the physical effects of the surgical operation were far outweighed by the social and moral implications of abortion in this social class.

Threat was rated as mild, moderate or severe. The *duration of effect* of events was rated as 'short term' if effects lasted for less than a week, and 'long term' if they continued for more than a week. Similarly, in the case of difficulties short term ratings implied a duration of 4 weeks to 6 months, and long term more than 6 months. Positive events were not included in this study, though certain experiences, such as marriage, childbirth or promotion in one's job, were judged in the context of the life situation of the individual rather than by their superficial 'positive' connotations. For example, a junior school teacher with more than adequate qualifications for a higher post, applied under pressure from her family for the post of headmistress of a secondary school, and was appointed. The demands of this job were largely administrative and quite new to her. The additional loss of contact with young children, whom she had enjoyed teaching, were stresses she saw as far out-weighing the advantages of a rise in income. She was willing to resign her new job, but could not, as there was no guarantee of getting another job. This situation was rated as a long term job related difficulty.

The assessment of 'threatfulness' was made by considering both the respondent's view as well as an estimation of 'contextual threat' (Brown and Harris, 1978). This is a concept designed to eliminate the effects of illness on a respondent's evaluation of her world, as other-wise reports of events which had occurred even a year prior to the interview would tend to be greatly coloured by the presence of psycho-logical distress at the time of the interview. Self-reports of threat-fulness could not, however, be totally ignored, as they were necessary as guidelines. The widely differing life experiences of the various social classes in India, modified by regional cultural differences and urban-rural distinctions, make it extremely difficult for an investigator from one class to make an unbiased judgement about the quality of experience of a subject from another class. To illustrate, in Bengali middle and upper classes financial debts sit heavily upon one's shoulder, being considered as evidence of failure or incompetence or worse. On the other hand, both males and females from the lower class perceived debts as an everyday aspect of life and did not see any reason to condemn those who incurred debts. It was a common phenomenon to find that families with a total monthly income of Rs. 40 or so, had incurred debts of over thousand rupees, and these debts had often accumulated over many months with the family regularly borrowing money to buy provisions or even to make payments for a plot of land.

Ratings were made jointly by the author and a colleague who had not been present at the interviews and could therefore make an unbiased judgement which was not affected by the respondent's personality or mental state. The event or difficulty was assessed in the light of the particular life circumstances of the subject. A series of anchoring examples were used as guidelines.

CLINICAL EVALUATION OF 'CASE-NESS'

A small sample of out-patients was interviewed jointly by the author and the Consultant Psychiatrist at the Institute (Professor Chakraborty), in the manner just described, and ratings for the PSE items, clinical diagnosis and severity of illness were made so as to highlight the areas of possible major disagreement or difficulty with rating. However, none were found, and the interviews in the main study were conducted by the author alone. Ratings made for 30 women in the hospital sample were compared with the Consultant's separate assessments of the same women and no major differences were found. The same criteria for rating were used in the community sample. Clinical assessment of illness severity was determined by a rating of case/non-case, based on whether the person, had she consulted a psychiatrist, would have received psychiatric treatment or not. Explanations for the observation that women in the community sample whose symptoms had reached case severity, yet who had not sought treatment, will be discussed later. Great care was taken to ensure that these judgements of severity were made in a similar manner for the hospital and community samples. The use of the IRS as a screening instrument with a threshold score of 2, yielded a second 'borderline' between cases and non-cases. Using this method, 30 women in the out-patient sample and 37 women in the community sample were identified, and further investigations were made using the PSE. Additional ratings of 'mild', 'moderate', 'severe', or 'subclinical' were made based on the investigators' clinical evaluation.

STATISTICAL TESTING FOR SIGNIFICANCE

Chi-square (X^2) tests were used, with Yate's correction being applied, if any set of observations was smaller than five.

OBSERVATIONS AND RESULTS

Since the main purpose of the study was to compare clinical symptoms between the two groups of cases, with the diagnosed or established OPD cases of neurosis as paradigm, no emphasis was laid on demographic details. The groups were not matched, but close similarities were found between them in terms of factors like age and marital status. On the other hand, there were large discrepancies in social class distribution and education, as upper class and educated women did not attend hospitals. The community sample was specifically chosen to represent all the social classes, as it was believed that symptoms may vary according to class. Emphasis was laid on personality factors, as they affect symptoms. Only broad outlines of these features are mentioned here, as the details are not relevant to this presentation.

All 30 out-patients and 37 of the 180 women in the community sample scored 2 or more on the Individual Report Schedule (IRS) and were administered the PSE. The remaining 143 non-symptomatic women in the second group formed a control group for comparison of symptom patterns and stress factors. The other 37 women identified by the IRS are described as 'community cases' in the following tables; however, 7 of these 37 women were given a rating of 'subclinical severity' by the investigator and were therefore not truly 'cases' by clinical standards. This issue will be discussed later.

The majority of the OPD cases showed traits of obsessionality and anxiety-proneness in their premorbid personality. In only 20 per cent of the cases was there evidence of a normal, well-adjusted personality. Of the 30 out-patients initially diagnosed by the clinic Consultant as suffering from neurotic disorder, 2 women received a different diagnosis in this study, namely, neurotic personality disorder based on a more detailed enquiry into the antecedent personality and life circumstances. Of the 180 women in the community sample 52 per cent showed no evidence of neurotic personality traits, 12 per cent reported psychological distress; while 70 per cent of those with premorbid neurotic traits reported similar levels of symptoms.

ELABORATION OF THE FINDINGS

Finding (1): The Relation between Psychiatric State and Physical Complaints

While no individual in the hospital sample suffered from major physical problems that might be attributed to organic illness (such as hypertension, diabetes mellitus, pulmonary infections), 14 per cent of the community sample who merited a psychiatric case status did so, with similar problems seen in a smaller group of normals.

'Minor' physical complaints, such as weakness, body ache, dizziness and vague musculoskeletal pains, were reported by one third of the hospital sample and over half of the community cases. However, a substantial number of normals also reported such minor physical symptoms.

Enquiry into gynaecological symptoms and symptoms related to menstruation revealed that complaints pertaining to white discharge and scanty bleeding were most common. Where detailed enquiries revealed little evidence of pathology, the former complaint was included with the minor physical complaints. Of the 24 pre-menopausal women in the hospital patient group (the remaining 6 were menopausal or post-menopausal), one-third complained of scanty or irregular menstruation.

A smaller percentage of the community cases and normals had similar complaints (22 per cent and 27 per cent respectively). Nine of the community cases were menopausal or post-menopausal as compared to 26 of the normals, one was pregnant in the former group and two in the latter.

Finding (2): The Relation between Psychiatric State and Sleep Disturbance

Half of the hospital sample suffered from major sleep disturbances. Sleep problems were significantly more common among those in the community with psychiatric distress (about 60 per cent) than among normals (nearly 20 per cent), (p. <0.01).

Table 1 The number of life events of each type occurring in the year preceding the onset of psychiatric symptoms, or in the case of normals in the year preceding the interview, showed that interpersonal and socio-sexual events were more common among those with symptoms in both samples, five of the hospital patients reported childbirths in the year under study.

Finding (3): The Distribution of Life Events in Hospital and Community Samples

As far as the mean number of life events were concerned, there was no difference in the three groups of subjects, but there was a highly significant excess of events among those with psychiatric symptoms in the community as compared to normals, 53 per cent of whom reported no life events (p. <.01).

TABLE 1
Life Events in Hospital and Community Samples
(Figures indicate number of events in each group)

Type of Life Event	Hospital Sample	Community Sample	
		Cases	Normals
	30	37	143
Education Related	4	2	6
Job Related	1	2	3
Interpersonal	4	5	—
Socio-sexual	9	10	8
Personal Health	2	3	11
Health—Other	—	3	6
Financial Loss	1	3	7
Bereavement	3	• 11	25
Child Related	1	5	5
Childbirth	5	—	13
Other	1	5	7
Total Number of Life Events	31	49	91

Table 2 showed the number of each kind of difficulties experienced during the year preceding the onset of symptoms, or the date of interview in the case of those who did not have any psychological symptoms. As in the case of life events, certain types of difficulties were not frequently associated with morbidity, viz., interpersonal, financial, child related and personal health difficulties.

TABLE 2
Difficulties in Hospital and Community Samples
(Figures indicate number of difficulties in each group)

Type of Difficulty	Hospital Sample	Community Sample	
		Cases	Normals
Education Related	—	—	2
Job Related	1	4	14
Interpersonal	8	14	41
Socio-sexual	1	—	4
Personal Health	5	5	27
Health—Other	—	4	28
Financial	4	11	32
Child Related	1	6	22
Other	3	10	27
Total Number of Difficulties	23	54	197

Finding (4): The Distribution of Difficulties in Hospital and Community Samples

Difficulties were more common in the community sample; a slightly higher mean number of difficulties was reported by the group of normal women. However, 60 per cent of hospital cases reported at least one difficulty, while 87 per cent of community cases and 74 per cent of community normals did so.

Finding (5): The Relationship between the Duration and Severity of Life Events and Morbidity in the Community Sample

This observation indicated a significantly higher association of certain types of events with psychological morbidity in the community sample namely, events with negative long term effects (lasting at least one week), particularly those rate as moderate to severe in the degree of threat caused. Five life events were rated 'positive' among the cases and 20 life events among the normals.

Finding (6): The Relationship between the Severity of Difficulties and Morbidity in the Community Sample

Difficulties (which, by definition, were stresses lasting at least 4 weeks) were significantly more common among cases than among normals in the community sample, particularly when the severely distressing ones were considered. There were no significant differences in effect, when difficulties were divided into those lasting less than 6 months and those more than 6 months (p. <0.05).

Finding (7): The Relationship of Social Class with Life Events and Difficulties in the Community Sample

Significant differences were observed in the class distribution of life events and difficulties, with higher rates of events in the upper two classes. While difficulties were most common in the lowest social class. The probability level was less then 5 per cent for both.

Finding (8): The Relationship of Marital Status and Life Events/Difficulties in the Community Sample

A lower frequency of stress was observed among single women; 57 per cent of this group reported no life events and 35 per cent reported no difficulties. On the other hand, a significantly higher frequency of difficulties was observed among women who were either widowed, separated or divorced (p. <0.05).

TABLE 3
Duration of Symptoms in Hospital and Community Samples

Duration of Symptoms	Hospital Cases (N = 30)	Community Cases (N = 37)
Less than One Month	18 (60%)	14 (38%)
One Month to One Year	2 (7%)	12 (32%)
Over One Year	10 (33%)	11 (30%)

TABLE 4
Severity of Symptoms in Hospital and Community Samples

Severity of Symptoms (Clinical Rating)	Hospital Cases (N = 30)	Community Cases (N = 37)
Mild	13%	51%
Moderate	43%	27%
Severe	44%	3%
Sub-Clinical	0%	19%

Tables 3 and 4 revealed a pattern of more chronic but milder conditions in the community sample, i.e., 30 per cent had symptoms for over a year, and in 19 per cent they were not of sufficient severity to warrant a rating of 'caseness'. In contrast, 60 per cent of the hospital sample reported the onset of symptoms within a month, but 87 per cent suffered moderate to severe distress due to these symptoms.

Table 5 showed the frequency of the ICD-9 sub-types of neurotic disorders diagnosed in 30 women in the hospital sample and 37 women in the community sample who reported at least two symptoms on the Individual Report Schedule (screening instrument) and were therefore only loosely labelled 'cases'. Seven (19 per cent) women in the latter group were, in fact, judged not to be suffering from neurotic illness of case severity.

TABLE 5
ICD-9 Diagnostic Groups in Hospital and Community Samples

ICD-9 Diagnosis	Hospital Cases (N = 30)	Community Cases (N = 37)
Anxiety State	20%	46%
Neurotic Depression	10%	16%
Obsessive-Compulsive Disorder	23%	—
Hysteria	13%	—
Hypochondriasis	7%	—
Neurasthenia	—	3%
Other (+ Somatisation Disorder)	20%	—
Neurotic Personality	7%	16%
Sub-Clinical Severity	—	19%

Two women in the hospital sample (7 per cent) and six women (16 per cent) in the community 'case' group had symptoms of a mixed nature which had persisted for many years, thus fitting a description of neurotic personality disorder rather than any of the discrete sub-types of neurosis.

Of the ICD-9 diagnoses, anxiety state was observed in almost half the community cases. A greater variety of diagnoses was seen in the hospital sample, with almost equal numbers of anxiety state, obsessive-compulsive disorder and 'other' neuroses. The last category included 2 women who were suffering from chronic pain with no organic basis, and 3 women who had multiple physical complaints affecting several body systems, but with no discernible physical basis.

TABLE 6
CATEGO Classes (Derived from PSE-CATEGO) in Hospital and Community Cases

CATEGO Classes	Hospital Cases (N = 30)	Community Cases (N = 37)
(ON) Obsessional Neurosis	20%	8%
(ND) Neurotic Depression	43%	62%
(RD) Retarded Depression	30%	3%
(AW) General Anxiety State	—	5%
(PN) Phobic Anxiety	3%	19%
(HT) Hysteria	3%	—
(YW) Other Neuroses	—	3

Table 6 indicates that all the subjects satisfied the criteria for

CATEGO classes of the neurotic disorders; 73 per cent and 65 per cent of women among the hospital and community cases respectively were rated as suffering from non-psychotic depressions (ND) and retarded depression (RD). Obsessive-compulsive disorder in the hospital group and phobic anxiety in the community group were the second most frequent diagnostic sub-types.

TABLE 7
Frequency of PSE Items in Hospital and Community Cases

PSE Item	Approximate Percentage Frequency	
	Hospital Cases (N = 30)	Community Cases (N = 37)
Physical Health (Subjective Evaluation)	87	70
Worrying	53	78
Tension Pains	77	41
Tiredness	73	35
Muscular	30	19
Restlessness	57	32
Hysterical Conversion	50	14
Nervous Tension	80	65
Free-floating Autonomic Anxiety	40	38
Anxious Foreboding	30	32
Panic Attacks	30	11
Situational Autonomic Anxiety	53	24
Autonomic Anxiety on Meeting People	—	5
Specific Phobias	20	24
Inefficient Thinking	50	30
Poor Concentration	80	59
Neglect Due to Brooding	43	27
Loss of Interest	77	46
Depressed Mood	77	65
Hopelessness	67	38
Suicidal Plans/Acts	7	5
Morning Depression	70	54
Social Withdrawal	30	5
Self Depreciation	27	—
Lack of Confidence with People	23	—
Simple Ideas of Reference	13	19
Guilty Ideas of Reference	10	5
Pathological Guilt	3	—
Poor Appetite	47	16
Delayed Sleep	33	46
Subjective Anergia	77	30
Early Waking	27	30

Table 7 (Contd.)

PSE Item	Approximate Percentage Frequency	
	Hospital Cases (N = 30)	Community Cases (N = 37)
Loss of Libido	27	5
Premenstrual Exacerbation	43	19
Irritability	77	57
Obsessional Checking/Repeating	40	27
Obsessional Cleanliness	47	16
Obsessional Ideas/Rumination	30	27
Depersonalisation	7	—
Lost Emotions	3	—
Fugues/Blackouts/Amnesias	3	—
Dissociative States	13	5
Conversion Symptoms	47	5
Impairment of Memory	20	24
Good Insight	53	76
Poor Insight	47	24
Social Impairment	97	38

Table 7 While nearly all the hospital cases complained of social impairment as a result of the symptoms, just over one-third of the community cases did the same. Over half of the former group and three-fourths of the latter group retained good insight into the psychological nature of their problems. None of the women reported expansive mood, ideomotor pressure, grandiose ideas/actions, derealisation or delusional mood. The most common traits in the hospital sample were subjective evaluation of poor physical health, nervous tension, tension pains, irritability, poor concentration, as well as a complex of 'depressive' symptoms, viz., depressed mood, loss of interest, subjective anergia (all occurring in over 75 per cent of these women). The field cases reported all the symptoms less frequently, the most common being worrying, subjective evaluation of poor physical health, nervous tension and depressed mood (over 60 per cent).

While 133 women of the community sample of 180 women showed evidence of 'somatisation' (i.e., somatic complaints of no discernible organic basis), 102 women were not psychologically ill (i.e., no evidence of neurotic symptomatology of 'case' severity). However, of those who could be diagnosed as neurotic, 89 per cent showed some degree of somatisation.

TABLE 8
Somatisation in the Community Sample

Somatisation	Community Sample	
	Cases (N = 37)	Normals (N = 143)
None	5 (11%)	41 (29%)
Present	31 (89%)*	102 (71%)**

* 14 per cent of these had concurrent physical illness.
** 23 per cent of these had concurrent physical illness.

Several women in both groups, cases and normals, had concurrent physical illnesses, for which objective evidence was available. Symptoms of these illnesses were clearly differentiated from those rated as manifestations of somatisation.

TABLE 9
Relationship Between Somatisation Scores and Neurotic Symptom Scores (IRS) in the Community Sample

Community Sample Somatisation Score (0–12)	Neurotic Symptoms Score (IRS)		
	0	1–2	3+
0	43%	16%	13%
1–2	36%	39%	26%
3 +	21%	45%	61%
		p. <0.01	

TABLE 10
Relation between Social Class and Somatisation in the Community Sample

Social Class	Community Sample Somatisation Scores	
	0	1 +
Upper + Upper Middle (97	31%	69%
Lower Middle (43)	39%	61%
Lower (40)	12%	88%
		p. <0.02

Table 10 showed that a significantly greater number of women in the lowest class somatise whereas fewer women in the other two groups

did so. However, it is interesting to note that the proportions were far from negligible (69 per cent in the upper and upper middle classes taken together).

DISCUSSION

The aim of this study was to examine the modes of presentation of minor psychiatric disorder ranging from clear-cut neurotic syndromes that easily fit into the diagnostic sub-types, through forms manifesting mixed symptomatology, to those that are perhaps better described as personality disorder. We also intended to examine closely the sub-clinical or borderline forms of the disorder with the intention of delineating the possible factors that determine which individual will develop an illness of case severity, and to highlight the vulnerability factors in such individuals. For this purpose, we studied neurotic symptom patterns and other evidence of psychological distress, such as somatisation, in a sample of hospital patients and a large number of women in the community, some of whom had evidence of such distress, but had not sought psychiatric help. The original study was also motivated to explore the extent to which unreported community cases resemble fully developed clinical ones and the influence personal and social factors, in the form of life events and difficulties, have on the genesis of clinical syndromes. Only a brief and modified account has been presented here, omitting most of the social variables for various reasons, the shortcoming of the sampling being the crucial one.

The community sample of 180 women included 24 women who were diagnosed as suffering from neurotic disorders of case severity, and another 6 who complained of similar degrees of psychological distress related to personality disorder. This gives a morbidity rate of 15 per cent which is comparable to the rate from the community study mentioned earlier. A greater proportion of women in the 45–60 years age group were ill, followed by those in the 26–35 years age group, thereby indicating an increasing rate of morbidity with advancing age. Though women who were widowed/separated/divorced formed a small group, they reported the highest rates of illness, followed by married women. Both these findings were consistent with those of the CMDA survey (1983).

Symptom Patterns

Symptom patterns may be considered under the headings of physical and psychological symptoms; the former including physical complaints that had a possible basis in organic dysfunction of some sort, and those without any evidence of organic dysfunction which were, therefore, rated as symptoms of somatisation. Psychological symptoms are described in terms of PSE items and include disturbances of sleep.

As indicated by Finding 1, psychological distress among the community sample was accompanied by a higher frequency of 'major' physical complaints due to organic causes. This association between physical and psychiatric problems has also been reported by Shepherd *et al.* (1981). When the tables on somatisation (Tables 8 and 9) were examined, an interesting feature emerged, that is, a high proportion of those without overt psychological symptoms complained of physical discomfort, though they were outnumbered by those with similar problems who were also psychologically distressed. Furthermore, Table 9 showed that those with more neurotic symptoms somatised more, thus contradicting the view of somatisation as a method of expression of distress among those described either as alexithymic or as limited by language (Leff, 1981) or sophistication to express their discomfort in psychological terms. The belief that somatisation is most common among the lowest socio-economic classes has been reported by other authors (Janakiramaiah and Subbakrishna, 1980), and was borne out by our findings, though it was far from negligible in the other classes. The phenomenon of 'somatisation' in many eastern cultures, and 'psychologisation' in middle class western cultures were investigated in great depth by Kirmayer (1984). Closer examination revealed that psycho-social problems were expressed in somatic terms in almost all cultures, and this may be viewed as a mode of medical help-seeking. However, a substantial proportion of women in the community who had not sought help in the past nor wished to do so, expressed somatic complaints, though this behaviour may be seen partly as a response to being interviewed by a doctor. Studies in other countries have reported the presence of discrete syndromes that are manifested along with particular configurations of bodily symptoms, such as *shinkeishitsu*—a Japanese form of neurasthenia *hwa-byung*—a syndrome among Korean women, and *brain fag* in Nigeria, which were nevertheless seen by the parent culture as disorders with psycho-social causes. That physical treatments were more often sought and received from both doctors and healers was not necessarily evidence of denial of emotional causes, but rather indicated the absence of an exaggerated separation of the 'body' from the 'mind'. It is more likely that certain cultures favour a greater use of figurative and metaphoric expressions of distress in terms of bodily symptoms, and thus allow the individual to respect a social code that values group harmony above individual emotional expression (Tanaka-Matsumi and Marsella, 1976).

This explanation fits in well with our experience of the detailed enquiry into areas of personal and family conflict among Bengali patients. Besides, individual personality factors may account for greater reporting of physical symptoms by the heightened states of arousal and increased sensitivity to autonomic sensations in some individuals (Akiskal, 1983), and cultural factors in turn may influence sensitivity to visceral sensations as well as their excessive expression. It has been suggested (Chakraborty and Sandel, 1985) that 'too much' somatisation may be due to the absence of taboo in Indian culture regarding talking about one's body.

Bodily complaints related to gynaecological symptoms were examined (Finding 1) and it was found that menstrual problems (menorrhagia, dysmenorrhoea, or scanty menstrual flow) were reported by cases as well as by normals. Complaints of 'white discharge' (leucorrhoea) were also included in this group. As the total number was relatively small, statistical testing was not possible, but the impression was that these complaints were more severe among those characterised as neurotic personality types. A 'pre-menstrual tension syndrome' associated with high neuroticism scores has been reported by western scholars with a greater frequency among married women than among single women (Coppen and Kessel, 1963). However, the present study did not detect any syndromal association of affective symptoms and bodily distress that could be related to the pre-menstruum. Regarding psychological distress at the time of menopause, 2 of 7 menopausal women, and 7 of 28 postmenopausal women in the present study had such complaints, the proportions being only slightly higher than in the case of pre-menopausal women (27 cases among 142 women, excluding those who were pregnant). Menopause is a period of 'psycho-social transition' and there are widespread changes in endocrine function, physical appearance and social roles, some of which are functions of age rather than the physiological status. Jai Prakash and Murthy (1981) have observed an increase in morbidity at menopause, with a subsequent decline after it. However, Guttentag *et al.* (1980) could find little evidence of this in their review of the subject.

An interesting observation was the frequency of childbirth in the year preceding the onset of illness in the hospital sample—5 women in a group of 30 women reported this, and 4 of these women developed obsessive-compulsive neurosis following childbirth. Similar findings were reported by Dutta (1979).

Table 7 presents a detailed account of the distribution of PSE items in cases in the two samples. As the majority of community cases had not sought treatment, this indicates the kind of distress that may induce a person to seek medical help. Hypochondriasis, expansive mood, ideomotor pressure, grandiose ideas and actions, derealisation, depersonalisation, fugues/amnesia, dissociative states and conversion symptoms occurred very rarely in the community sample. The two symptoms relating to guilt were also uncommon and this feature has been observed earlier among Indian patients, especially among depressive ones (Venkoba Rao, 1978; Hoch, 1968). Simple ideas of reference, though rare, were almost equally common in both hospital and community groups. This confirms the findings of another study in Calcutta that reported a high rate of persecutory beliefs and paranoid symptoms in normal persons, as well as in psychotic and neurotic patients (Bhattacharya, 1981).

Symptoms like worrying, anxious foreboding, delayed sleep and early waking (items of little diagnostic discriminatory power) were more common in cases in the community. On the other hand, symptoms like inefficient thinking, poor concentration, neglect due to brooding, loss of interest, social withdrawal, lack of confidence with people and self-depreciation were more common among the hospital cases. These were often associated with high self-ratings by the individuals of 'social impairment' and 87 per cent of this sample was clinically judged to be moderately to severely ill (Table 4). Few community cases reported these symptoms, only 38 per cent reported 'social impairment' and correspondingly only 30 per cent had illnesses of moderate to severe degree.

Morning depression, suicidal plans, loss of weight due to poor appetite and early waking which are considered to be characteristic of severe or 'psychotic' depression were fairly common in the cases in this study. Impairment of memory, though not listed as a neurotic symptom in the PSE, but rather as an indicator of organic defect, was reported by patients in both groups. In most cases it accompanied anxiety and, in these women, it could have been a result of their inability to concentrate.

As indicated by Finding 2, sleep disturbances were common among all cases, and those with psychological distress were significantly more affected, though 13 per cent of normals also complained of severe sleep problems. Sweetwood *et al.* (1980) reported a strong association between sleep disturbances and psychological symptoms, but only a weak association between sleep disturbances and life change scores, thereby implying that stress only disturbs sleep where circumstances are sufficiently pathogenic to cause the formation of other symptoms.

The diagnostic breakdown of the hospital sample was compared with that derived from records of all neurotic patients seen at the out-patient clinic in the year 1982. The latter group included 28 per cent anxiety state, 20 per cent obsessive-compulsive disorder, 20 per cent hysteria, 16 per cent neurotic depression, and 11 per cent other psychoneuroses and was similar to the figures given in Table 14 for the hospital cases.

As indicated in investigations of the natural history of neurosis, the majority remit often spontaneously. Harvey-Smith and Cooper (1970) found that the illnesses often ran an episodic course with the most favourable outcome for depressive and psychosomatic conditions, and the least for anxiety and mixed affective disorders. This is reflected in Table 3 in the difference between the more acute, severe cases that were seen at the clinic, and the longer lasting forms, milder in degree perhaps due to a natural process of resolution, that were contained in the community.

Life Stresses

The study of life stresses revealed several significant trends. First, while large numbers of both hospital and community cases experienced life events and difficulties (Findings 3 and 4), the latter group reported more of these. Also, high proportions of normals reported equivalent degrees of stress—47 per cent of normals had faced at least one life event and 74 per cent had experienced at least one difficulty. More significantly, 81 per cent of cases in the community reported both events and difficulties, while the difference in the percentages of hospital cases and normals that had the same were not so markedly different. Second, more severely threatening events of long term effect and difficulties of greater severity were significantly more common among community cases than among normals, and the greater the total number of such stresses, the greater was the association with illness. Similar findings have also been reported by other authors (Paykel *el at.*, 1980), but some have failed to find any relationship; the studies, however, often had marked methodological differences. Third, whether these stresses were causally related to the illness or dependent upon the abnormal mental state was examined by including only those stresses which could be clearly dated as preceding the symptoms, or the nature of which excluded the possibility of the individuals having contributed in some way to the circumstances. Often respondents were vague about the details of separate events, particularly about the duration of effect, and this was more common in the lower social class. So as to avoid accidental over-reporting, due to the inclusion of stresses that occurred more than a year before the onset of the illness, this study chose to omit the vaguely defined stresses. Consequently, somewhat lower rates of stress may have been obtained than that seen in reality, particularly in the lowest class (Finding 7). However this class experienced significantly higher number of difficulties (62 per cent with 2 or more) while 30 per cent of the highest class faced 2 or more life events (only 10 per cent of the lowest faced the same). Schless *et al.* (1977) have explained the lack of positive correlation between events and illness among those who live with a continually high level of stress; for such people individual stresses may be relatively insignificant.

That marital status is related to levels of stress (Finding 8) was perhaps not unexpected, and may have been the mediating factor linking marital status with psychological morbidity in women. It was seen that 96 per cent of the widowed/separated/divorced experienced more than one difficulty, and 61 per cent had more than one life event. This group was followed by the married group who faced higher degrees of stress than single women.

Observations related to life circumstances provided an interesting lead that was not examined in as much detail as it warranted. While normals reported a higher mean number of difficulties (Finding 4) and almost an equal mean number of events (Finding 3) as cases, they did not succumb to these stresses. Furthermore, several community subjects with 'sub-clinical' psychological distress faced more stress than the cases. (Mean number of events—1.6 in community normals,

1.1 in community cases; mean number of difficulties, 2 in community normals, 1.1 in community cases.) Though personality variables were not examined in detail, data indicated traits of anxiety proneness or obsessionality to be common among the symptomatic group.

Thus it appeared that cases in both samples were largely similar in qualitative symptomatology, while differing in severity and in rates of those symptoms that reflected this dimension. In general community cases have a longer duration, but are less severe in degree. That life stress seems to be relatively less frequent among the severely affected hospital sample may point to the vulnerability factors that remain to be discovered by future workers as do the protective factors operating among the group of highly stressed yet asymptomatic women.

Conclusions

The main finding in this study was that cases of clinical severity were found in the community which were often unreported and untreated. Though the hospital sample had more severe forms of illness, cases in the community were more often mild in degree and more likely to be chronic. The clinical symptom patterns, especially the core group of anxiety related ones, were similar in the two groups. Persons characterised as neurotic personality types were overrepresented in the hospital sample.

The study of life events and difficulties revealed certain interesting but ambiguous features. While stress in the form of severely threatening life events and difficulties preceded the onset of psychological distress significantly more frequently, it was found that a high proportion of normals and persons with sub-clinical symptoms reported markedly threatening life circumstances as well. This finding pointed to the existence of coping mechanisms that enabled the inhabitants of one of the most stressful cities of India to function reasonably well in the face of constant hardships. Our experience during the course of detailed interviews of women of all social classes pointed to a certain style of acceptance. Though they struggled continually against poverty, illness, housing problems, and the particular pressures faced by women caught in a conflict between traditional roles and the demands of present-day urban life, women in the less advantaged classes rarely felt that these were issues one should complain about.

As the samples were not representative of the population, no inferences could be drawn about the rates of illness or the demographic character of the symptomatic group. However, the differential effects of employment in the social classes is an interesting contrast to the reports of morbidity in industrialised western countries.

A few words may be added regarding the instruments used in the study. The Present State Examination of Wing *et al.* (1974) was translated into Bengali and its applicability tested in a Bengali population. As workers in other cultures have observed (Swartz *et al.*, 1985), this instrument has a number of disadvantages which need to be modified to suit cross-cultural requirements. The Individual Report Schedule, a locally developed screening instrument, tried in the community sample proved to be easy to administer and rate; used with a threshold score of 2 in a community study, it yielded a reasonably low false positive rate of about 10 per cent.

Appendix I

The Family Report Schedule

(English version of the questionnaire in Bengali.
Questions were modified for conversion into codes.)

Section I Identification as in fascimile.
II Demographic information of each member of the household.
III Particulars of each member of the household: Reported by informant.

(III)
    Particulars
(Yes—1, No—2)

Serial number of household members as in column 1 of section II.

        Sl. No.   (1)   (2)   (3)   (4)   (5)

1. Born with mental/physical defects.
2. Illness of mother at pregnancy or birth of this person.
3. Milestones delayed:
   a Started walking later than others.
   b Started talking later than others.
4. Mentally retarded.
5. Performance in school (well—1, not well—2).
6. If 2 for question 5, reasons (naughtiness—1, forgetfulness—2, dullness—3, restlessness—4).
7. Suffers from fits.
8. For children under 14 years, write appropriate code applicable:

      a Very intelligent
      b Very naughty
      c Would not study
      d Runs away from home or school
      e Stammers
      f Very lazy
      g Too quiet
      h Fights and quarrels
      i Any other (specify/see manual)

9. Assessment code by Supervisor.
10. Remarks, if any (Investigator/Supervisor).

Section (IV)	Particulars of each member of the household over the age of 13 years

---

Sl. No.   (1)   (2)   (3)   (4)   (5)

(IV) Particulars
(Yes—1, No—2)

A. Major achievements in the family (Record comments).
B. Exceptional/successful member.

1. Political worker/leader.
2. Got into trouble with law (Comments in remark—item 21).
3. Disappeared from home.
4. Became a *sadhu*.
5. Gets *thakur-bhar*.
6. Has *suchi-bai*.
7. Loss of memory/*bhimroti* (For persons above 60 years of age).
8. Consumes a Alcohol.
             b Drugs.
            (Comments in item 21)
9. Remains depressed/does not work/does not talk.
10. Suspicious nature—*Sandeho-Batik*.
11. Personality features (Character type).
    a. Asocial.
    b. Irritable.
    c. Violent.
    d. Suspicious.
    e. Depressed.
    f. Talkative.

    g. Too jolly.

    h. Shouts and breaks.

    i. Any other (see manual).

12. Unusual behaviour

    a. Muttering.

    b. Laughing.

    c. Refusal to work.

    d. Irrelevant talk.

    e. Wanders around.

    f. Does not eat/eat anything.

    g. Neglects appearance/remains dirty.

    i. Any other (see manual).

Sl. No.	(1)	(2)	(3)	(4)	(5)

(IV) Particulars

13. Mental illness.

14. Unnatural death (accident—1, suicide—2).

15. Advice sought for any complaints (Yes—1, No—2).

16. If 'yes' to question 15, for which complaints (write item numbers of this block).

17. Advice sought from doctors—1, healer—2, knowledgeable person—3, others—4.

18. Advice necessary for any complaints (yes—1, No—2).

19. If 'yes' to questions 18, for which complaints (write item numbers of this block).

20. Assessment codes (Not for Investigators/Supervisors).

21. Remarks (For Investigators/Supervisors.
                Write verbatim account. Your own comment, if any, should be clearly marked).

Section (V) Social particulars of the household as reported by the informant.

1. Friendly neighbourhood.

2. Good family relations.

3. Regular performance of religious ceremonies.

4. Observation of pollution rules (mostly—1, partly—2, not at all—3).

5. Assessment (not to be filled by the investigators).

6. Remarks.

Section (VI) Family type—Nuclear/Extended/Joint/Single Member
                              (1)   (2)   (3)   (4)

Section (VII) Candour and co-operation—Good/Fair/Indifferent/
Uncertain   (1)   (2)   (3)
                                              Uncertain
                                                  (4)

Appendix II

The Individual Report Schedule

(English version of the questionnaire in Bengali.
Questions were modified for conversion into codes.)

Section (VIII)   Identification
Section (IX)   Recreation
  1. Goes out for purposes of recreation (yes—1, no—2).
  2. Takes part in group activities (yes—1, no—2)
     (e.g., membership of a club).
  3. Recreation at home (yes—1, no—2).

Section (X)   Duration to be recorded as per instruction Code
  4. Presence of: Yes—1
                                                         No—2

        a. Aches and pains.
        b. Burning sensation.
        c. Stomach trouble.
        d. Headache, giddiness, jammed feeling.
        e. Weakness.
        f. Palpitations.
  5. Problems with sleep (disturbed sleep).
  6. If 'yes' to question 5,
        a. Difficulty in falling asleep.
        b. Early waking.
  7. Gets fits, faints or becomes unconscious.
  8. If 'yes' to question 7 (frequently—1, infrequently—2) (see
     manual).

9. Average duration (days—1, hours—2, minutes—3) (record actual duration in days, hours and minutes in duration column).
10. *Coding (not to be filled by the investigator).*
    Section (VIII)
11. Difficulties in concentration.
12. Worrying too much.
13. Feeling 'nervous' and anxious recently.
14. Feeling tense and restless recently.
15. *Coding (not to be filled by the investigator).*
16. Suffers from palpitation, sweating and suffocation at the same time.
17. Cleans and washes excessively.
18. Thoughts go round and round in the mind.
19. Needs to check action frequently.
20. Intense fear of anything (e.g., falling ill, fainting in the street, mad people, contracting serious diseases, any other).
21. *Coding (not to be filled by the investigator).*
22. Feels sad and depressed without reason.
23. Lost interest in everything.
24. Feels helpless and inadequate at times.
25. *Coding (not to be filled by the investigator).*
26. Advice sought for any complaints.
27. If 'yes' to question 26, for which complaints (write item number of this block).
28. Advice sought from (doctor—1, knowledgeable person—3, others—4).
29. Advice necessary for any complaints.
30. If 'yes' to question 29, for which complaints (write item number of this block).
31. *Coding (not to be filled by the investigator).*
   Remarks (Respondent's remarks to be written verbatim. Investigator's remarks to be clearly marked).

Appendix III

The Validity of the Individual Report Schedule

Dr. B. Sandel, DPM, MD(Psych), MRC(Psych)

The IRS was devised for use as a screening instrument in a community survey of psychiatric morbidity aimed at identifying neurotic disorders. Therefore, it was required to be sensitive enough to detect subjective distress of severity sufficient to warrant therapeutic intervention, whether physical or psychological, though the results were expected to depend upon the threshold score specified as well as upon the population being examined. Other important requirements of such a schedule are the ease of administration and a simple system of scoring. This instrument has been used by lay interviewers with a brief period of training and has been found to fulfill these requirements.

In order to assess the ability of the IRS to detect neurotic syndromes of clinical severity, we have examined the correlation of case severity as detected by a threshold score of 2 on the IRS with clinical assessment of case severity and diagnosis by the PSE-CATEGO system (Wing *et al.*, 1974).

A hospital population of 30 patients (diagnosed by a senior psychiatrist to be suffering from neurotic disorder of case severity) was administered the IRS, and was also examined using the PSE. All subjects scored above 2 on the IRS and received a diagnosis of one of the CATEGO classes of neurosis. Clinical assessment by the author suggested that all subjects suffered from distress of 'case' severity and two of these women had neurotic personality disorders which contributed to this distress. This dimension of 'personality' was also available from the IRS.

When examining a community sample of 180 women, the results were somewhat different, as the IRS was now truly used as a screening instrument. A group of 37 women scored above 2 and all were diagnosed, according to the CATEGO system, as suffering from neurotic disorder. However, clinical assessment by the author resulted in seven of these 37 women receiving ratings of 'sub-clinical' severity of symptoms, i.e., these were 'false positives' detected by both the IRS and the PSE-CATEGO.

Another group of six women of the 37 women were clinically determined to be suffering from case-level symptoms which were, however, due to the marked effects of a neurotic personality type.

Thus, the findings indicate that the IRS, used with a threshold score of 2, is a highly sensitive indicator of psychological distress with a false positive rate of about 10 per cent (7 'sub-clinical' syndromes among a total of 67 persons with neurotic syndromes of widely varying severity) when compared with assessment by clinical interview, but with 100 per cent positive correlation with a standardised diagnostic system such as the CATEGO (used with the PSE).

It must be added that the IRS is more appropriate in the context of Indian psychiatry as it is interviewer rated and does not necessitate a long period of training if used by non-medical interviewers. It is also easily translatable into Bengali, as in this study, and the selection and phrasing of items such as these are easily understood by the local population.

CALCUTTA METROPOLITAN DISTRICT

STATEMENT SHOWING MUNICIPALITIES, NON-MUNICIPAL URBAN UNITS AND MOUZAS FALLING WITHIN THE CALCUTTA METROPOLITAN DISTRICT BOUNDARY

MUNICIPALITIES

1. Magra
2. Bansberia
3. Polba
4. Chinsurah
5. Chandannagar
6. Bhadreswar
7. Champdani
8. Baidyabati
9. Serampore
10. Chanditala
11. Bally
12. Domezur
13. Sankrail
14. Uluberia
15. Panchla

16. Budge Budge
17. Maheshtala
18. Behala
19. Sonarpur
20. Baruipur
21. Bhangar
22. Tollygunj
23. Rajarhat
24. Dum Dum
25. Barasat
26. Khardaha
27. Titagarh
28. Jagaddal
29. Naihati
30. Bijpur
31. Kalyani

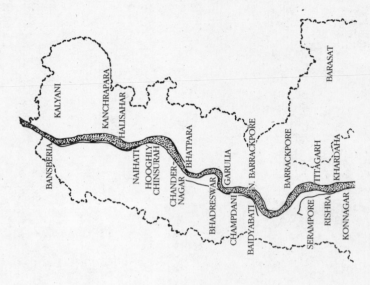

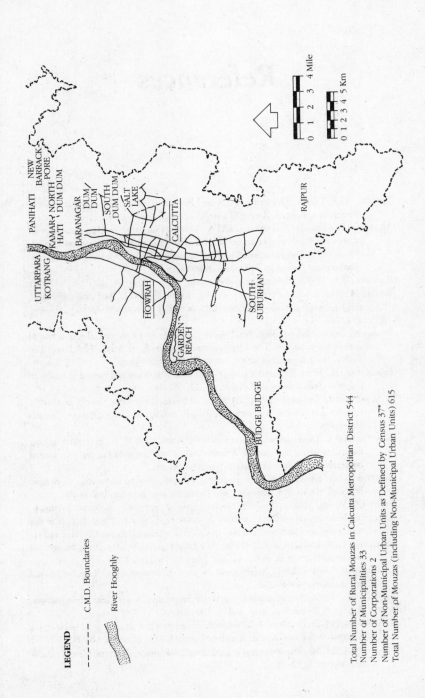

LEGEND

– – – – – C.M.D. Boundaries

River Hooghly

UTTARPARA KOTRANG

PANIHATI NEW BARRACK PORE

KAMAR HATI NORTH DUM DUM

BARANAGAR

DUM DUM

SOUTH DUM DUM

SALT LAKE

CALCUTTA

HOWRAH

GARDEN REACH

SOUTH SUBURHAN

RAJPUR

BUDGE BUDGE

0 1 2 3 4 Mile

0 1 2 3 4 5 Km

Total Number of Rural Mouzas in Calcutta Metropolitan District 544
Number of Municipalities 33
Number of Corporations 2
Number of Non-Municipal Urban Units as Defined by Census 37*
Total Number of Mouzas (including Non-Municipal Urban Units) 615

References

AKISKAL, H.S. (1983). Dysthymic disorder: Psychopathology of proposed chronic depressive sub-types. *American Journal of Psychiatry*, 140 (1), 11–20.

AMERICAN PSYCHIATRIC ASSOCIATION (APA). (1968). *Diagnostic and Statistical Manual of Mental Disorders—II Edition*. Washington: American Psychiatric Association.

————. (1980). *Diagnostic and Statistical Manual of Mental Disorders—III Edition*. Washington: American Psychiatric Association.

BAGADIA, V.N. (1987). Personal communication.

BEISER, M., RAVEL, J.L., COLLOMB, H. and EGETHOFF, C. (1972). Assessing psychiatric disorder among the Serer of Senegal. *Journal of Nervous and Mental Disorders*, 154, 141–51.

BELMONT, LILIAN. (Ed.). (1984). *Final report: Screening for severe mental retardation in developing countries*. The International Pilot Study of Severe Childhood Disability. Serie Research Cahiers Geestelijk Gehendicapten.

BHASKARAN, K., SETH, R.C. and YADAV, S.N. (1970). Migration and mental ill-health in industry. *Indian Journal of Psychiatry*, 12, 102–16.

BHATTACHARYA, DEBASHIS. (1981). A study of persecutory ideas among psychiatric patients and general population in Bengali culture. M.D. dissertation, Calcutta University.

BHATTACHARYA, DEBASHIS and CHAKRABORTY, AJITA. (1987). Role conflict among Bengali working housewives: A field study. Paper presented at the 39th annual conference of Indian Psychiatric Society, Calcutta.

BHATTACHARYA, DEBORAH. (1986). Pagalami: Ethnopsychiatric knowledge in Bengal. Maxwell School of Citizenship and Public Affairs, Syracuse University.

BROWN, G.W. and HARRIS, T. (1978). *Social origins of depressions*. London: Tavistock.

CALCUTTA METROPOLITAN DEVELOPMENT AUTHORITY (CMDA). (1983). Report of the health and socio-economic survey in Calcutta Metropolitan Area. Vols. I and II.

CARSTAIRS, G.M. and KAPUR, R.L. (1976). *The great universe of Kota: Stress, change and mental disorder in an Indian village*. London: Hogarth Press.

CHAKRABORTY, AJITA. (1967). A critique of the concept of mental health. *Indian Journal of Psychiatry*, 9, 192–202.

————. (1970). Ethnic variation in drug responses: A rejoinder. *Transcultural Psychiatry Research Review*, Vol. 7, 100–101.

————. (1972). Problem of the mentally disordered in Calcutta. In S. Sinha (Ed.), *Cultural profile of Calcutta*. Anthropological Society of India, 120–31.

————. (1978a). Migration and urbanization problems in Calcutta. *Mental Health and Society*, 5, 72–78.

CHAKRABORTY, AJITA. (1978b). A short screening instrument for detection of neuroses in field surveys. Unpublished.

—————. (1982). Guidelines for out-patient treatment with psychotropic drugs. Paper presented at the 34th annual conference of the Indian Psychiatric Society, Madras.

—————. (1974). Symbolism of dirt: Psychopathology of pollution. Paper presented at 26th Annual Conference of Indian Psychiatric Society, Bangalore.

—————. (1985). Mental health of migrants in Calcutta. In P. Pichot, P. Berner and R. Wolf (Eds.), *Psychiatry: State-of-the-art*. Vol. 8. New York: Plenum Publishers.

CHAKRABORTY, AJITA and BANERJI, G. (1975). Ritual, a culture specific neurosis and obsessional states in Bengali culture. *Indian Journal of Psychiatry*, 17, 211–16, 273–83.

CHAKRABORTY, AJITA and SANDEL, B. (1985). Somatization syndrome in Calcutta. In P. Pichot, P. Berner and R. Wolf (Eds.), *Psychiatry: State-of-the-art*. Vol. 8. New York: Plenum Publishers.

CHAKRABORTY, AJITA and BHATTACHARYA, DEBASHIS. (1985). Witchcraft beliefs and persecutory ideas in Bengali culture. *Indian Journal of Social Psychiatry*, 1, 231–43.

CHANDRASHEKAR, C.R. (1981). A victim of an epidemic of possession syndrome. *Indian Journal of Psychiatry*, 23, 370–72.

CHANDRASHEKAR, C.R., VENKATARAMAIAH, V., MALLIKARJUNAIAH, M., NARAYANA REDDY, G.N., and VASUDEVA RAO, C.K. (1982). An epidemic of possession in a school in South India. *Indian Journal of Psychiatry*, 24, 295–99.

CHODOFF, P. (1974). The diagnosis of hysteria: An overview. *American Journal of Psychiatry,* 131, 1073–78.

CLIFFORD, W. (1966). *A review of social casework in Africa*. Nairobi: Oxford University Press.

COLLIS, R.J.M. (1967). Physical health and psychiatric disorder in Nigeria. *Transcultural Psychiatry Research Review*, 4, 153–55.

CONKLIN, GEORGE H. (1968). The family formation process in India. *Journal of Family Welfare*, 14, 28–37.

COPPEN, A. and KESSEL, N. (1963). Menstruation and personality. *British Journal of Psychiatry*, 109, 711–721.

DOHRENWEND, B.P. (1975). Socio-cultural and socio-psychological factors in the genesis of mental disorders. *Journal of Health and Social Behaviour*, 16, 365–72.

DUBE, K.C. (1970). A study of prevalence and biosocial variables in mental illness in rural and urban community in U.P., India. *Acta Psychiatrica Scandinavica*, 46, 327–59.

DUTTA, D. (1979). A clinical evaluation of 57 cases of obsessional neurosis. *Indian Journal of Psychiatry*, 21, 316–19.

FARIS, R. and DUNHAM, H. (1960). *Mental disorders in urban areas*. New York: Hafner.

FINNEY, JOSEPH C. (Ed.). (1970). *Culture change, mental health and poverty*. New York: Simon & Schuster.

FOULDS, G.A. (1976). *The hierarchical nature of personal illness*. London and Toronto: Academic Press.

FREEMAN, H. (1984). *Mental health and the environment*. New York: Churchill Livingstone.

GELDER. M., GATH, D. and MAYOU, R. (Eds.). (1983). *Oxford textbook of psychiatry*. London: Oxford University Press.

GELDER, M.G. (1986). Neurosis: Another tough old word. *British Medical Journal*, 292, 972–73.

GIEL, R. (1975). Problems of assessing the needs of the population. In T.A. Baasher,

G.M. Carstairs, R. Giel and F.R. Hassler (Eds.), *Mental health services in develop ing countries.* Geneva: WHO.

GOLDBERG, DAVID P. (1972). *The detection of psychiatric illness by questionnaire.* London: Oxford University Press.

GRUENBERG, E.M. (1965). A review of mental health in the metropolis, the midtown Manhattan study. *International Journal of Psychiatry,* 1, 77–85.

GUTTENTAG, M., SALASIN, S. and BELLE, D. (1980). *The mental health of women.* New York: Academic Press.

HARVEY-SMITH, E.A. and COOPER, B. (1970). Patterns of neurotic illness in the community. *Journal of Royal College of General Practitioners.* 19, 132.

HIGGINBOTHAM, HOWARD N. (1979). Culture and the delivery of psychological services in developing nations. *Transcultural Psychiatry Research Review,* 14, 7–27.

HOCH, E.M. (1968). Contents of depressive ideas in Indian patients. *Indian Journal of Psychiatry,* 3, 28–34; 120–24.

JAI PRAKASH, I. and MURTHY, V.M. (1981). Psychiatric morbidity and the menopause. *Indian Journal of Psychiatry,* 23, 242–46.

JANAKIRAMAIAH, N. and SUBBAKRISHNA, D.K. (1980). Somatic neurosis in Muslim women in India. *Social Psychiatry,* 15, 203–6.

KALA, A.K., SINGH, G., KURUVILA, K., GUPTA, L.N., WIG, N.N. and SETHI, B.B. (1986). Acute psychosis—ICMR multicentred study. Paper presented at the 38th conference of the Indian Psychiatric Society, Jaipur.

KAPUR, PROMILA. (1970). *Marriage and the working woman in India.* Delhi: Vikas Publishing House.

KAPUR, R.L., KAPUR, M. and CARSTAIRS, G.M. (1974). Indian Psychiatric Interview Schedule (IPIS). *Social Psychiatry,* 9 (2), 61–70.

————. (1974). Indian Psychiatric Survey Schedule (IPSS). *Social Psychiatry,* 9 (2), 71–76.

KAPUR, R.L. and PANDURANGI, A.K. (1979). A comparative study of reactive psychosis and acute psychosis without precipitating stress. *British Journal of Psychiatry,* 135, 544–50.

KENDELL, R.E. and ZEALLEY, A.K. (1983). *Companion to psychiatric studies.* Third edition. London: Churchill Livingstone.

KESSLER, RONALD C. (1979). Stress, social status and psychological distress. *Journal of Health and Social Behaviour,* 20, 259–72.

KIRMAYER, L.J. (1984). Culture, affect and somatization. *Transcultural Psychiatric Research Review,* 21, Part I, 159–88; Part II, 237–62.

KREITMAN, N. (1961). The reliability of psychiatric diagnosis. *Journal of Mental Science,* 107, 876–86.

LANGNESS, L.L. (1976). Hysterical psychosess and possessions. In W.P. Lebra (Ed.), *Culture-bound syndromes, ethnopsychiatry and alternate therapies.* Honolulu: University of Hawaii Press.

LEFF, J. (1981). *Psychiatry around the globe—A transcultural view.* New York: Marcel Dekker.

LEIGHTON, A.H. (1959). *My name is Legion.* New York: Basic Books.

LEIGHTON, A.H., LAMBO, T.A., HUGHES, C.C., LEIGHTON, D.C., MURPHY, J.M, and MACKLIN, D.B. (1963a). *Psychiatric disorder among the Yoruba.* Ithaca: Cornell University Press.

LEIGHTON, A.H., HARDING, H.S., MACKLIN, D.B., MacMILLAN, A.H. and LEIGHTON, D.C. (1963b). *The character of danger: Psychiatric symptoms in selected communities.* New York: Basic Books.

LIN, TSUNG-YI. (1953). A study of the incidence of mental disorders in Chinese and other cultures. *Psychiatry*, 16, 313–36.

LISHMAN, W.A. (1978). *Organic psychiatry*. Oxford: Blackwell.

MACPHERSON, STEWART. (1983). Mental illness in the third world. In Philip Bean (Ed.), *Mental illness: Changes and trends*. London: John Wiley.

MAUSNER, JUDITH S. and BAHN, ANITA K. (1974). *Epidemiology: An introductory text*. Toronto/London: W.B. Saunders.

MAYER-GROSS, W., CROSS, K.W., HARRINGTON, J.A., SREENIVASAN, U. (1958). The chronic mental patient in India and in England. *Lancet*, 1, 1265–67.

MAYER-GROSS, W., SLATER, E. and ROTH, M. (1954). *Clinical psychiatry*. First edition. London: Cassell.

MEHTA, PANKAJ, JOSEPH, A. and VERGHESE, A. (1985). An epidemiological study of psychiatric disorders in a rural area in Tamil Nadu. *Indian Journal of Psychiatry*, 27(2), 153–58.

MITRA, A. (1986). The illusion of growth. *Telegraph* (Calcutta), Supplement, 5 October 1986.

MURPHY, H.B.M. (1977). Migration, culture and mental health. *Psychological Medicine*, 7, 677–83.

——————. (1982). *Comparative psychiatry: The international and intercultural distribution of mental illness*. Berlin/New York: Springer–Verlag.

——————. (1983). Socio-cultural variations in symptomatology, incidence and course of illness. In M. Shepherd (Gen. Ed.), *Handbook of psychiatry*. Vol. 1. Cambridge: Cambridge University Press.

MURPHY, H.B.M. and RAMAN, A.C. (1971). The chronicity of schizophrenia in indigenous tropical people. *British Journal of Psychiatry*, 118, 489–97.

NANDI, D.N., DAS, N.N., CHAUDHURI, A., BANNERJI, G., DUTTA, P., GHOSH, A. and BORAL, G.C. (1980). Mental morbidity and urban life: An epidemiological study. *Indian Journal of Psychiatry*, 22, 324–30.

NATHANSON, CONSTANCE A. (1980). Social roles and health status among women: The significance of employment. *Social Science and Medicine*, 14 A, 463–71.

NATIONAL MENTAL HEALTH PROGRAMME. (1981). Draft proposal by the Expert Committee. Directorate General of Health Services, India.

NOYES, A.P. (1955). *Modern clinical psychiatry*. Fourth edition. Philadelphia: W.B. Saunders Co.

PAYKEL, E.S., EMMS, E.M., FLETCHER, J. and RASSABY, E.S. (1980). Life events and social support in puerperal depression. *British Journal of Psychiatry*, 136, 339–46.

PETERS, LARRY G. and PRICE-WILLIAMS, DOUGLAS. (1983). A phenomenological overview of trance. *Transcultural Psychiatry Research Review*, 20, 5–39.

PLOG, S.C. (1969). Urbanization, psychological disorders and the heritage of social psychiatry. In S.C. Plog and R. Edgerton (Eds.), *Changing perspective of mental illness*. New York: Rinehart and Winston.

PRABHU, G.G., VERMA, N., JOHN, A., DANIEL, E. and ELIZABETH, C.K. (1985). Brochure. 7th World Congress of IASSMD, New Delhi.

PRINCE, R. (1968). World distribution and patterns of possession states. In R. Prince (Ed.), *Trance and possession states*. Montreal: McGill University Press.

RAMCHANDRAN, V., SARADA MENON, M. and RAMAMURTHY, B. (1979). Psychiatric disorders in subjects aged over fifty. *Indian Journal of Psychiatry*, 22, 193–98.

RUSSELL, G.F.M. and HERSOV, L.A. (1983). The neuroses and personality disorders. In M. Shepherd (Gen. Ed.), *Handbook of psychiatry*. Vol. 4. Cambridge: Cambridge University Press.

SANDEL, BEGUM. (1982). A comparative study of neurotic symptom patterns, life-stresses and demographic features in women of a local neighbourhood and women attending a psychiatric outpatients department. M.D. (Psychiatry) dissertation, Calcutta University.

SCHLESS, A.P., TEICHMAN, A., MENDELS, J. and DI GIACOMO, J.N. (1977). The role of stress as a precipitation factor of psychiatric illness. *British Journal of Psychiatry*, 130, 19–22.

SEN, B., NANDY, D.N., MUKHERJI, S.P., MISHRA, D.C., BANERJI, G. and SARKAR, S. (1984). Psychiatric morbidity in an urban slum dwelling community. *Indian Journal of Psychiatry*, 26, 185–93.

SETHI, B.B., GUPTA, S.C. and KUMAR, P. (1967). A psychiatric study of 300 urban families. *Indian Journal of Psychiatry*, 9, 280–302.

SETHI, B.B., GUPTA, S.C. MAHENDRU, R.K. and KUMARI, P. (1972). Migration and mental health. *Indian Journal of Psychiatry*, 14, 115–32.

SETHI, B.B., GUPTA, S.C., MAHENDRU, R.K. and PROMILA, K. (1974). Mental health and urban life: A study of 850 families. *British Journal of Psychiatry*, 124, 243–46.

SETHI, B.B. and MANCHANDA, R. (1978a). Socio-economic, demographic and cultural correlates of psychiatric disorders with special reference to India. *Indian Journal of Psychiatry*, 20, 199–211.

———. (1978b). Family structure and psychiatric disorders. *Indian Journal of Psychiatry*, 20, 283–288.

SHAH, A.M. (1973). *The household dimension of the family in India*. Calcutta: Orient Longman.

SHAH, A.V., GOSWAMI, U.A., MANIAR, R.C., HAJARIWALA, D.C. and SINHA, B.K. (1980). Prevalence of psychiatric disorders in Ahmedabad (An epidemiological study). *Indian Journal of Psychiatry*, 22, 384–89.

SHEPHERD, M. (1977). Beyond the layman's madness: The extent of mental disease. In J.M. Tanner (Ed.), *Developments in psychiatric research*. London: Hodder and Stoughton.

SHEPHERD, M., COOPER, B., BROWN, A.C. and KALTON, G. (1981). *Psychiatric illness in general practice*. Second edition. London: Oxford University Press.

SNAITH, P. (1980). *Clinical neurosis*. Oxford: Oxford University Press.

SPITZER, R.L., SHEEHY, M. and ENDICOTT, J. (1977). DSM III: Guiding principles. In V.M. Rakoff, H.B. Kedward and H.C. Stancer (Eds.), *Psychiatric diagnosis*. London: Macmillan.

SPITZER, R.L., WILLIAMS, J.B.W. and SKODOL, A.E. (1980). DSM III: The major achievements and an overview. *American Journal of Psychiatry*, 137: 2, 151–64.

SROLE, L., LANGNER, T.S., MICHAEL, S.T., OPLER, M.K. and RENNIE, T.A.C. (1962). *Mental health in the metropolis*. New York: McGraw Hill.

STEIN, ZENA and SUSSER, MERVYN. (1975). Public health and mental retardation: New power and new problems. In M.J. Begab and S.A. Richardson (Eds.), *The mentally retarded and society*. Baltimore: University Park Press, pp. 53–73.

SUSSER, MERVYN. (1973). *Causal thinking in health sciences*. London: Oxford University Press.

SWARTZ, L., BEN-ARIE, O. and TEGGIN, A.F. (1985). Subcultural delusions and hallucinations. Comments on the Present State Examination in a multi-cultural context. *British Journal of Psychiatry*, 146, 391–94.

SWEETWOOD, H., GRANT, I., KRIPKE, D.F., GERST, M.S. and YAGER, J. (1980). Sleep disorder over time: Psychiatric correlates among males. *British Journal of Psychiatry*, 136, 456–62.

TANAKA-MATSUMI, J. and MARSELLA, A.J. (1976). Cross-cultural variations in the phenomenological experience of depression. I. Word association studies. *Journal of Cross-Cultural Psychology*, 7, 379–96.

TEJA. J.S., KHANNA, B.S., and SUBRAHMANYAM, J.B. (1970). Possession in Indian patients. *Indian Journal of Psychiatry*, 12, 72–87.

THORLEY, A. (1986). In Peter Hill, Robin Murray and Anthony Thorley (Eds.), *Essentials of postgraduate psychiatry*. London: Grune and Stratton.

TOFFLER, A. (1970). *Future shock*. New York: Random House.

VENKATARAMAIAH, V., MALLIKARJUNAIAH, M., VASUDEVA RAO, C.K., and NARAYANA REDDY, G.N. (1981). Possession syndrome: An epidemiological study in West Karnataka. *Indian Journal of Psychiatry*, 23, 213–18.

VENKOBA RAO, A. (1978). Some aspects of psychiatry in India. *Transcultural Psychiatry Research Review*, 15, 7–28.

VERGHESE, A., BEIG, A., SENSEMAN, L.A., SUNDER RAO, S.S., and BENJAMIN, V. (1973). A social and psychiatric study of a representative group of families in Vellore town. *Indian Journal of Medical Research*, 61, 608–20.

————. (1974). Neuroses in Vellore town—An epidemiological study. *Indian Journal of Psychiatry*, 16, 1–7.

VERMA, L.P., SRIVASTAVA, D.K., and SAHAY, R.N. (1970). Possession syndrome. *Indian Journal of Psychiatry*, 12, 58–71.

WIG, N.N. (1982). Draft proposal for National Mental Health Programme. New Delhi: D.G.H.S.

WING, J.K., COOPER, J.E. and SARTORIUS, N. (1974). *Measurement and classification of psychiatric symptoms: An introductory Manual for PSE and CATEGO Programme*. Cambridge: Cambridge University Press.

WOOTTON, BARBARA. (1959). *Social science and social pathology*. London: George Allen and Unwin.

WORLD HEALTH ORGANIZATION. (1948). *WHO Constitution*. Geneva.

————. (1973). Schizophrenia. Report of an International Pilot Study. Geneva.

————. (1975). Organization of Mental Health Services in Developing Countries/ Promotion of National Health Services. Geneva.

————. (1978a). *Manual of the International Classification of Diseases, Injuries and Causes of Death*. Revision 9. Geneva.

————. (1978b). Mental disorders: Glossary and guide to their classification in accordance with the ninth revision of the International Classification of Diseases. Geneva.

————. (1978c). The application of advance in neurosciences for neurological disorders. Technical Report Series No. 629.

WHO/SEA. (1978). Mental health in South-East Asia: Mental retardation. (Development and Strengthening of Mental Retardation Programme. Report of a Workshop). SEA/Ment/45.

WHO. (1979). *Schizophrenia: An international follow-up study*. New York: John Wiley.

Index

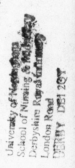